Boarding on

the State

– a candid account of the survival

and growth of England's

State Boarding Schools

John Haden

First published in Great Britain in 2015 by
Barny Books
76 Cotgrave Lane, Tollerton,
Nottingham NG12 4FY
Copyright © John Haden 2015

A CIP catalogue record for this book is available from
the British Library.

ISBN: 978-1-906542-77-1 in paperback print format
ISBN: 978-1-966542-8 in ebook format

Front Cover: The cartoon which the Times chose to illustrate
an article by the author in March 1993 is reproduced with kind
permission of the artist and Times Newspapers.

Line drawings by Keith Wragg
Photographs from the author's collection
Designed and typeset by Julian Bower Associates Ltd
Printed and bound by CPI Anthony Rowe Ltd, Chippenham

To all those who care for other people's children in
England's State Boarding Schools,
after the last lesson of the day has finished.

Contents

Preface

The world of boarding school is a mystery to most of us. We have never been a boarder and all the families we know send their children to day schools. What we think we know comes more from the fantastical world of Harry Potter or the repressed one of Goodbye, Mr Chips than the reality of UK boarding schools in the twenty first century. Old stereotypes harking back to Tom Brown's Schooldays and Mallory Towers may live on in our collective memory but they have little relevance to the day-to-day experience of today's families.

Those of us who have worked in good boarding schools know that such schools can provide positive and valuable experiences for both their pupils and their staff. They can provide a richer curriculum both in the classroom and beyond than their day school equivalents and opportunities to establish friendships which can last a lifetime. But we also have to accept that boarding is not for all children. Amongst the majority of young people who are very happy to be boarders, there are some who have been deeply unhappy in boarding for a whole host of reasons, many beyond the control of the school. Schools have to be especially vigilant in their care of all boarders and the Children Act 1989 has transformed our thinking about ensuring that safeguards are in place.

There was a time when UK boarding seemed to be in decline. Today, boarding schools have not only survived but are in the news for positive reasons. The number of state schools with boarding provision is growing for the first time in fifty years. Dotted about across England and Wales are about forty state maintained schools which have provision

7

for boarders. They are successful and popular with parents. Their results on any measure from examination results to sporting excellence are impressive. Ofsted rates many of them as 'outstanding schools'. These state schools share many of the attractive characteristics of good boarding schools in the UK independent sector, with the obvious difference that none of them charge fees for teaching and learning.

The great majority of today's boarders are the children of loving parents who want the best for their family. But some children do not have that huge advantage. They may be in the care of Local Authorities. The minimal life-chances of such 'looked after children' is recognised as a national scandal. The need to make better provision for our most disadvantaged young people has led many to look again at what boarding schools could offer. Both major parties are interested in developing boarding places at the State's expense for these children. They are convinced by the positive outcomes and lower costs of such places for the handful of children that now benefit from such provision. Many more should have the opportunity to succeed that most boarders now take for granted

But why were state boarding schools established and why are they still partly funded from public money? Why, in recent years, have new boarding facilities been opened in state schools which have no tradition of boarding? Why have famous independent boarding schools like Wellington and Eton sponsored new boarding opportunities in the UK state sector? Why have a handful of independent schools with boarders chosen to transfer to the state sector and how have they done so? Why do teaching and non-teaching staff choose to live and to work in these schools and why do parents choose such schools for their children?

To try to answer these questions, I have drawn on my own experience as a boarder at school, as a student teacher in a boarding school, of working as a teacher and boarding house Tutor in my first job followed by four years working in a Ugandan State Boarding school at the time of Idi Amin. After returning to England, I had the privilege of being the Head of two very different UK State Boarding schools and through that becoming the Chairman first of the State Boarding Schools' Association (SBSA) and then our parent body, the Boarding Schools' Association (BSA).

When our younger son chose to become a boarder at his State school, we became boarding parents. When I left headship, I worked as an Adviser supporting Heads and Governors in State schools with boarders. Having been trained as an Ofsted Inspector, I was asked by the Department for Education (DfE) to serve as an independent member of the Board of ISI, the Independent Schools Inspectorate. When ISI developed a new Inspection framework to bring together the inspection of school and boarding into one integrated report, I was asked to chair their working party of boarding Heads.

For fifty years I have had the privilege of working in or with such schools. This book is firstly a memoir of that experience, warts and all, distilled from fifty years of diaries and focusing on the schools I know best. To protect the identities of pupils, I have referred to individuals by their first names only, and all of these have also been changed. Where appropriate, names of adults have also been changed. Secondly, it is an attempt to collect together the stories of the boarding houses and their schools in membership of

SBSA today. I have drawn on what schools have said about themselves on their web-sites or what Ofsted has reported in public. I hope that this will avoid misunderstandings. This is not a 'good schools guide', although it celebrates many very good schools. The third part of this book is about people, the teachers and others who make boarding houses and schools work well, the parents who choose to send them to our schools and the boarding pupils who provide their schools with every sort of challenge.

The 2015/6 school year will see both the 25th anniversary of the founding of the SBSA and the 50th anniversary of the founding of BSA. It is a good time to give account of the role of State Boarding Schools, of the benefits we can offer to children and their parents, to demonstrate by anecdote and statistics that we can support children from a wide variety of backgrounds including some of the most vulnerable children in the UK. We know that by helping these children and their families, we can enhance both individual life chances and general social mobility.

It is now over fifteen years since I last told a boarder to tuck his or her shirt in. I hope that distance has allowed a degree of candour and that I may be forgiven for any indiscretions in my attempt to celebrate England's State Boarding schools and the staff who make them possible.

John Haden 2015

1. Why boarding and why state?

Madame Dubois was puzzled. She had come with the French Exchange party to spend ten days in our Lincolnshire state school. She had discovered that we had boarders.

'But why?' she asked. 'Is this not a school for the children of the town? And the farmers in the countryside, do they not have cars?'

For her, and she said most French families, it was simply incomprehensible. Why would loving parents send their children away to school? There was only one reason she could think of. It must be a strange English form of child abuse.

'For your Queen, yes,' she said, having visited Windsor and crossed the Thames to see Eton, where the Queen sent her Grandsons to school.

'If you live in a castle, you must send your children to a grand school. We have visited the College at Eton. That I understand. But for the people, why do they need boarding? Perhaps their children are being punished. Perhaps they have behaved very badly?'

Two weeks later, just as we were starting a boarders' leave weekend when our boarders left us for two nights at home, the Dutch Cricket Team arrived. They had come to play our first XI and other local schools. Their short tour was one product of a friendship between our Head of PE and one of their teachers. Their school had hosted our cricketers many times over the years in a very happy arrangement, with the added frisson that few people knew that the Dutch even played cricket.

After a few nights with their host families, most of the Dutch XI moved into our boys' boarding house for the weekend, supervised by their teachers. When the school week started and our boy boarders returned, the Dutch boys moved back to their host families. Their teachers agreed that it was very helpful to have a boarding house which could be used in this flexible way, although there was no boarding tradition in their schools.

Later that year, two of the Dutch boys returned, not as cricketers, but as full boarders. Their parents visited our school to check that what they had heard was true. If students could move within Europe to access University courses outside their own country, this should be possible at secondary school level. They were pleased to discover that one little known spin-off of the Treaty of Rome was the opportunity to send their sons to take their A levels in an English state school. If they could achieve good A level grades, they could then go on to best UK universities.

To these pragmatic Dutch parents, the opportunity for their sons to board with us at a third the cost of a place at an English independent school was just too good an opportunity to miss. Their boys were fluent in English and also in German. They could complete a post-16 course in two years and go to university for a three year degree. It was not a question of why – more a matter of why not? So began the 'Euro-boarder' arrangements which have brought a steady trickle of able and highly motivated young people into our State Boarding schools although, as Madame Dubois had pointed out, most were set up as schools for the local community and some have been fulfilling this role since the Middle Ages.

It is not just the French who are puzzled by the concept of boarding at a state school. A fellow State Boarding Head once described how difficult it was to explain to those he met just what his role was. Some misheard; his favourite was the lawyer who specialised in personal injury claims. She advised him to get good insurance cover and make sure that all pupils wore helmets and knee pads. She thought he had said that he ran a skate-boarding school. Most refused to believe that State Boarding schools existed. English boarding schools were, of course, private schools.

For the great majority of UK adults, 'boarding' is synonymous with 'Independent' – something you paid for because it was the family tradition or because you wanted the best for your child or to avoid sending your children to the local state school. The fact that schools with boarding places could also exist within the state-funded education system has been described as 'education's best kept secret'. But there are such schools today in almost every part of England and they include examples of almost every type of UK state school. Their number is small, currently just under forty, but for the first time since the 1950s, that number is now growing. Collectively, they provide about five thousand boarding places in schools where all the costs of teaching and learning are paid by the State.

~

The English have been sending sent their sons away to school for a very long time, since the start of the Christian church in these islands. When St Augustine established his monastery at Canterbury in 597 AD, the monks encouraged Anglo-Saxon families to send them their sons to receive an education to prepare them for the priesthood. When King Henry VIII closed Augustine's monastery, he re-founded the monastery school as King's School, Canterbury. It claims to be the oldest school in the world, having been in continuous existence for over fourteen hundred years. The school remained the local grammar school for boys from Canterbury and the surrounding part of Kent until the 1870s when it followed other similar schools to become a 'Public School'.

But Augustine was not the first evangelist to reach the British Isles. Irish monks led by St Columba established a monastery on the Scottish island of Iona in 563, thirty four years earlier than that at Canterbury. From Iona, St Aidan, was sent to Lindisfarne, off the coast of Northumbria, to establish a monastery there in 634 AD. Thus, the Christian Church in England has had from the earliest days two roots, the southern Roman root of Canterbury and the northern Celtic root of Lindisfarne. Both provided boarding education for boys.

There are no Northern England schools which can rival King's Canterbury in antiquity but some are not far behind. From Lindisfarne, St Cuthbert travelled south and west to Carlisle and established a monastery there in 685. Within that community a school was established which survived to become Carlisle Grammar School which eventually became today's Trinity School, Carlisle. Although it has retained its strong link with Carlisle Cathedral, this state school no longer offers boarding places.

Another Saxon churchman, St Wilfrid, also came south from Lindisfarne to become the Abbot at Ripon on the edge of the Yorkshire Dales where he built an abbey in 672. The school which was part of Ripon's Abbey community eventually became Ripon Grammar School. In common with most town grammar schools, Ripon had periods of growth and of decline. In 1820, the number of boys dwindled to a low point of just seventeen. Bristol Grammar School actually lost all its day boys at one point at roughly the same time,

14

although the Headmaster continued to receive his salary! Ripon's headmaster's solution to falling rolls was to expand the number of fee-paying boarders to about fifty, greatly outnumbering the day boys from the town.

Ripon Grammar School might have become an independent school, just as King's Canterbury had done. The citizens of Ripon fought a campaign to retain their 'free grammar school' as established by the Royal Charter of Catholic Queen Mary I, and they won. The school remained the grammar school for the town and the surrounding rural area. It still has that role today, offering selective day places to boys and girls who live within its catchment area. The school could therefore claim to be over thirteen hundred years old but has settled for a more modest four hundred and fifty years. It does still celebrate its earlier roots in Anglo-Saxon England in its Old English Motto: *Giorne ymb lare y diowatdomas* (Eager to learn and seek after righteousness).

Ripon Grammar School has survived every cataclysmic change in English history – the coming of the Normans to Anglo-Saxon England, the closure of the monasteries under Henry VIII and the bloody Catholic rebellions of the North of England against Protestantism under Edward VI and Elizabeth I. In the last fifty years, it has even survived all the attempts by the British Labour Party in Government to re-organise the nation's grammar schools into non-selective comprehensives. According to his wife, Labour's Tony Crosland had vowed to 'destroy every f...ing grammar school in England, Wales and in Northern Ireland', but he failed to destroy Ripon Grammar School.

North Yorkshire County Council introduced comprehensive schools in most areas of the County except just two. In Ripon and in Skipton, the grammar schools which had overwhelming local support were retained. Then in 2000, the Labour Party in power made another attempt to close the small number of surviving grammar schools. They gave parents in areas which were still selective the right to have a ballot to decide the issue. Ripon was the first and only selective school community in England to hold such a ballot. They chose to remain selective.

Like many grammar schools in rural areas, Ripon offered places to boys who could travel daily into the school on horseback from the surrounding rural area. Those who were too far away could be offered boarding places. In many towns, this arrangement had the added benefit for the Headmaster in that such additional pupils could be housed in the spare rooms at the top of the house provided for him. Their parents could be charged 'capitation fees' for board and lodging, a useful supplement to the meagre salary which the governors of most of the schools provided.

At Ripon, from 1962 when the boys' Grammar School combined with Ripon Girls' School to form a large mixed grammar school, boys and girls live in two separate boarding houses. The boys are still in the main school building of 1928, modernised for comfortable residential use. In 2015, the Governors are investing £1.2 million to provide an additional twenty one boarding places, mainly for girls. Currently, the school has applications from more girls who meet the selection criteria than there are girls' boarding places. This will be the first expansion of boarding at the school for a very long time. Parents in Yorkshire do still choose to send their children to this state school as boarders.

They send them to Ripon for four main reasons. Firstly, the school is selective. If you live in Harrogate or Helmsley,

Northallerton or Knaresborough your local secondary schools will today all be comprehensive, admitting pupils of the full range of academic ability. They may be good schools with good examination results and Ofsted Reports, but they are not selective. Parents of those children who can pass the 11+ for admission to a grammar school may still want their children to attend such a school. Ripon Grammar School has that status and there is a growing interest in such schools.

Secondly, Ripon Grammar has boarding places for both girls and boys. Both sexes from one family can be together at school. Having boarding houses opens up the opportunity to many more families from a very wide area to join the school. All day pupils have to live within a small catchment area but boarders can come from all over Yorkshire and beyond. They have to take the same 11+ assessment as day pupils and the minimum standard set for admission is the same for boarding as for day. The only limit is the availability of places.

Thirdly, there is the question of cost. Education is free at Ripon Grammar School as it is state-funded but the boarding houses are funded from fees paid by parents. The attraction is that these fees are a fraction of the equivalent in the independent sector. Ripon Grammar School charges about £9,000 per year compared with between £22,000 and £32,000 for boarding places in the region's independent schools. Many parents who have traditionally chosen independent boarding education for their children have become increasingly interested in State boarding for this third reason, because for many families, it is affordable.

The fourth reason is related to parental employment. Some parents have jobs which frequently take them away from home in the UK or abroad. Weekly boarding in schools like Ripon Grammar School can provide such families with stability for their children, an excellent academic education and the opportunity to make strong friendships at a fraction of the cost of the independent sector. They have the additional advantage that the school is serving the able children from all backgrounds in a community rather than just those of the most affluent. In today's more egalitarian society, the fact that State Boarding schools are not the preserve of a very affluent elite is a real attraction.

The first of these reasons apply to the one hundred and fifty five grammar schools in England which have survived to date but admit day pupils only. There are a further nine grammar schools scattered across England which have both boarding and day places. Ripon Grammar School is the only one in Yorkshire.

About fifty five miles across the Pennines to the west of Ripon is another very fine school, Lancaster Royal Grammar School. Not as old as Ripon and educating boys only until the 6th Form, Lancaster RGS exists to provide academic and sporting excellence for the boys of North Lancashire.

The school began not in a monastery but through the generosity of a succession of Lancaster men. Started by a miller some time in the C13th and re-endowed in succeeding centuries, it was not until Queen Victoria granted a charter in 1851 that it became the Royal Grammar School. Like Ripon, there have been boarders at the school for a very long time, and today there are two hundred boarding places for boys, organised in four houses with provision for Y7 and 8, for Y9, and in two houses for years 10 to 13. With a major grant for improvements in 2008, boarding accommodation at Lancast RGS is all of exceptionally high quality, matching the school's execellence in academic achievement and sport. The current Head is confident that the school offers 'an outstanding alternative to the independent sector'. With all the leading Northern grammar schools, including Leeds, Manchester and Newcastle, now in the independent sector, and none of them offering boarding, Lancaster RGS competes successfully in a very elite group of schools.

There are two more Royal Grammar Schools with boarders, at High Wycombe and at Colchester. Both admit boys only at eleven, as do Reading School and Adams Grammar School in Newport, Shropshire. Both Adams and Lancaster RGS have girls in the 6th form.

Skegness Grammar School in Lincolnshire, like Ripon, is mixed, as are the two Kent grammar schools with boarding places. Sir Roger Manwood's School at Sandwich admits boys and girls at eleven. Cranbrook School, one of the largest of the State Boarding schools, admits boys and girls at thirteen. Given the continuing interest amongst parents in selective education, such schools which can admit able pupils from a wide area as boarders would seem to have an assured future – provided that they continue to be allowed to select able pupils.

~

There are some Local Authorities where there is still strong support for selective schools and growing demands for more such schools. Kent still has over thirty grammar schools and there are plans to open a new satellite grammar school at Sevenoaks. Recent opinion polls show that there is still considerable support for grammar schools right across England, especially in London and the South East. Within the Conservative party, now in majority government, opinion on the issue is divided.

David Cameron is on record as saying that '*the whole grammar school debate is sterile and pointless.*' However, since saying that, and since winning the General Election, he has expressed much more positive views on grammar schools. Within the Conservative Party, Boris Johnson has become the strongest advocate for a return to selective education. His view remains that the decision to scrap grammar schools was '*a real tragedy for this country….I think they are a very important part of the mix in our educational system.*'

Meanwhile, the United Kingdom Independence Party (UKIP) adopted the policy that existing grammar schools should be allowed to remain while Labour remains implacably opposed to selective education. Prince Charles added his support to the pro-grammar cause by arguing in June 2014 that grammar schools '*provided poorer pupils with the opportunity to escape from their background*'. If this were true, providing more state grammar schools would offer more disadvantaged pupils with such a 'means of escape'.

Unfortunately for the Prince, the figures for disadvantaged children actually getting into a place at one of the one hundred and sixty four surviving state grammar schools in England do not support his case. Such schools remain almost exclusively the preserve of the affluent middle classes. Poorer families are kept out of their catchment areas by escalating house prices and by the growth of an expensive educational coaching industry which only the more affluent can afford.

The most recent research on access to grammar schools, carried out by Sir Peter Lampl's highly respected Sutton Trust, shows that just 3% of entrants to such schools are entitled to free school meals, the current best indicator of disadvantage. By contrast, 13% of entrants have come from fee-paying independent schools. The same research shows that an increasing proportion of entrants to grammar schools have come from Minority Ethnic families, as opposed to those who would classify themselves as White British. Some Asian and Chinese families and some Black and African families, all British and living in England, place a very high value on educational success and are prepared to invest in their children's future. The children of such families compete very successfully for grammar school places, but few are now socially disadvantaged by poverty.

~

Nine State Boarding schools are selective but they are a minority. Most State Boarding schools in England are non-selective. They are an eclectic collection. Several developed from former grammar schools which combined with the local secondary modern schools to form one school serving the whole local community. Typical of these is Steyning Grammar School in West Sussex which has also retained its 'grammar' name in spite of being a mixed comprehensive school. The school now offers 124 boarding places including a new purpose-built 6th Form House and celebrates boarding as a key part of what is a very successful large 11-18 comprehensive school. Their boarding provision has been judged 'outstanding' by Ofsted. Last year, 100% of boarding GCSE students achieved the bench-mark 5 A*-C grades and A level boarders achieved 100% pass grades.

The only state boarding school in Devon is the QE Academy Trust which chooses to celebrate its Academy status in its name, rather than its origins as the former Queen Elizabeth's School in Crediton. That school developed from the medieval boarding grammar school in the Devon town which was re-endowed twice under Edward VI and

Elizabeth I. It has continued the boarding tradition for hundreds of years and today offers fifty boarding places for boys and girls. It could call itself the '*Royal Grammar School, Crediton*', but instead has nailed its colours to the mast of modern comprehensive Academies.

One reason why parents may choose a particular school is its religious affiliation. English parents no longer send their young sons to monasteries to be trained for the priesthood but Catholic families in England can send their children to schools which were established by religious communities in the late 18th and 19th Centuries. The Jesuits established Stonyhurst and the Benedictines Downside and Ampleforth to provide Catholic families with boarding opportunities for their sons, all of which are now in the independent sector. Although there are many Catholic day state schools, there was only one, St Brigid's State School in North Wales, which had provision for boarders, but it is no longer open.

There are a several State Boarding schools which have a strong Anglican (Church of England) heritage, notably St George's School in Harpenden, north of London, Sexey's School in Bruton, Somerset and Shaftesbury School in Dorset. Other SBSA schools such as Wymondham College have a Christian ethos which is non-denominational.

~

Madame Dubois was puzzled – '*but why do the English send their children to boarding schools?*'

She believed that this did not happen in France. But she was wrong. In some very rural areas, French schools do have hostels for secondary school students to use during the school week where the problem of long daily travel means that they have a boarding need.

There is another recent development in France. Shortly after Nicholas Sarkozy became President, the French Government set up a number of '*Internats d'Excellence*' (Boarding Schools of Excellence). The first opened in 2009 in a former Army barracks in Sourdun near Provins supporting more than four hundred underprivileged children, as part of the '*Plan Espoir Banlieue*' ('Hope for the Suburbs Plan'). With financial support from the Total Oil Company and an enhanced revenue budget, the innovation was proving to be effective in enhancing student achievement. By 2013, forty five such schools had opened across France educating nearly twelve thousand students.

Sarkozy's vision for these 'Internats' was that children from disadvantaged backgrounds who show good academic potential, who did not have good study conditions at home, and could be easily distracted away from study, should be offered accommodation in boarding schools. What he envisaged was not '*austere as boarding school once was but modern........but 'boarding schools of excellence' where they would live and study.... taken care of completely during the week and benefit from school and educational support*'.

Sarkozy's scheme would be a good way to help families and offer children a more balanced life and above all enable able children to escape the pull of the street.

The introduction of these boarding schools was very much a reaction to the unrest in the poor suburbs of Paris, particularly in the '*banlieue*', areas like Clichy-sous-Bois, where there had been riots in 2005 and again more recently. But three years after these '*internats*' were introduced, Francois Hollande and the Socialists defeated Sarkosy and the whole boarding school programme came under review. It was said to be elitist, unreasonably expensive and with unproven outcomes.

The first closure of an '*Internat*', that at Cachan (Val-de-Marne) in September 2015, has been announced. Whether the others survive remains to be seen, but one cannot help but admire the vigour and scale of the French experiment involving thousands of pupils in hundreds of schools. In comparison, our UK developments look paltry. But would those of us who serve in England's State Boarding Schools be happy at seeing our schools converted into a solution to urban rioting?

2. Schools for people like us?

Some parents may choose schools for their children for religious reasons, but for most parents there are other concerns. In the Independent sector, both boarding and day, there is a strong tradition of social exclusivity. Some parents choose to send their children to schools which have pupils from families who share their social status, attitudes, values and assumptions – *'people who are like us'*. I first met this when I was eight, when my parents moved me from the warm bosom of my sisters' girls' school to the local Prep School, a much more challenging male world of Latin, caning and cricket.

Smartly dressed in my canary cap, yellow tie and school blazer, I met other local boys at the bus stop on our way to our different schools. I soon learnt that it was best to avoid the bus if I wanted to return home in the afternoon unbruised and still equipped with cap and tie. My parents relented and allowed me to cycle to school so that I could make a high speed exit from trouble. The school reinforced what my parents already accepted. There were two sorts of boy, the privileged elect in yellow caps and blazers and those disparagingly referred to as the 'VKs', the village kids.

So my parents sent me to Prep school to avoid me mixing in any way with the 'VKs' and they sent my sisters to the local day girls' independent school for similar reasons. We were happy to enjoy the benefits of this educational apartheid linked as it was for me to small classes, cricket and Latin. A small number of boys at the school were boarders from the age of eight. I felt sorry for them, cut off at least for the school week from their homes. I had no wish to become a boarder. But for many families we knew, boarding school was the natural choice after Prep school. It was what families like ours did and had been doing for a very long time, families which saw themselves as 'gentlemen and ladies'.

If parents choose independent schooling for social reasons, to ensure that their children associate only with their own social class, is that also true of boarding in the state sector? Put simply, are such schools for '*toffs*', just as Eton is perceived to be a school for '*toffs*', the theme of so many newspaper cartoons? The remaining State Boarding schools make no attempt to market themselves in terms of social exclusivity, choosing rather to focus on value for money. '*As good as, but one third the price*', is now the '*unique selling point*' of many such schools. With their boarding fees at around £10,000 per boarder, the second half of this claim is easy to verify.

Sexey's School, in its web-site section on fees, makes the claim explicit on behalf of all the other State Boarding Schools:

'*SBSA (State Boarding Schools' Association) schools provide high quality boarding at the lowest possible cost. Parents pay only the cost of boarding as the education at SBSA schools is free. This means that rather than paying £25,000+ a year for a place at an independent boarding school, you would probably be paying less than £10,000 a year at a State Boarding school.*'

The web-site goes on to point out that Sexey's is one of the best value for money boarding schools in the country having fees below most of the other State Boarding Schools! Competition by price is alive and well in SBSA.

~

In 2014, SBSA commissioned a survey of parental opinion to which over 1,500 parents of 4,300 boarders at 29 of the UK's State Boarding schools contributed. The results showed that 93% of these parents said their children were happy boarding, 95% of parents said they would recommend their child's school or boarding to others and over 80% of parents choose State Boarding schools because of *'high academic quality and the chance for children to fulfil their potential'*. It was the most ringing endorsement of the quality and customer satisfaction of State Boarding schools that has ever been carried out.

Parents, who can afford independent boarding places for their children, may choose to do so, but there is a growing conviction that such expense may not be either necessary or wise. SBSA claims that State boarding can be *'as good as'* what is offered in the independent sector, but is *'as good as'* justified? How can parents compare the quality of schools in the two sectors?

Boarding schools in the State sector are inspected and judged by Ofsted. Those in the Independent sector and in membership of the major Associations of that sector are inspected by the Independent Schools Inspectorate (ISI). The systems are quite separate, follow different criteria and make different judgments. The only effective overlap is that Her Majesty's Inspector of Schools issues an annual letter to ISI endorsing the quality of what ISI does.

In 2014, the Government's Department for Education (DfE) was widely reported as considering a major change to this inspection arrangement to bring the Independent sector, including the major Public Schools, into line with Ofsted Inspections for state schools. This could involve schools receiving an overall rating for quality, from outstanding to inadequate, and pupil progress measured in terms of national examination targets.

There was a predictably furious response from the Heads of these schools. The leaders of the Headmasters' and Headmistresses' Conference (HMC) which describes itself as 'a professional Association of Heads of the world's leading independent schools' decided to oppose such a change.

'Our overall aim is to slow down and then impede any policy moves designed to impose Ofsted methods, procedures and personnel on our schools.'

The Head of one HMC school expressed what his colleagues felt:

'ISI inspection is more focused on outcomes relative to the quality of pupils you're getting, but under Ofsted there is a lot of box-ticking, everyone is nervous of a system that is overly bureaucratic. People would be more comfortable if the government was making Ofsted a bit more like the ISI.'

It is tempting to comment – 'well, they would say that, wouldn't they!' – given that HMC is an exclusive club to which Heads of the leading independent schools are elected by their peers. It portrays itself as representing all that is of quality in British education although only just over 200,000 children attend their schools out of a national total of about 2.8 million secondary pupils, about 7%.

If it is as yet not possible to make direct comparisons of standards of provision within the two sectors, are there any ways of making objective comparisons? The annual publication of 'league tables', currently dominated by the independent and selective schools, demonstrates that schools which restrict their places to pupils of high academic ability can produce examination results which directly reflect that intake – hardly surprising!

Since 2014/5, the league table information has become even more difficult to interpret as the DfE chose both to include only results for examinations that were taken for the first time and to exclude the results of the International GCSE, IGCSE, examinations in their tables. This firstly disadvantaged some schools that had put pupils into GCSE early in Y10 as these results might not be as good as the pupil would achieve at the end of Y11. Secondly, Independent sector schools which use the IGSE and ignore GCSE found themselves with a result of 0%, provoking howls of protests from these schools. Whatever one might think of the Government's motivation for these changes, those schools which decide to operate independently of Government and then disdain to use the national Government approved examinations can hardly complain when the Government excludes them from the national league tables.

Much more interesting from a teacher's point of view is the notion of 'value-added'. This is an attempt to compare the educational achievement of a pupil at the point of entry to a school and the achievement of the same child at the point of leaving. A high 'value-added' score indicates that the school has enabled the child to make more progress than comparison with national averages would suggest. Schools with high 'value-added' scores have clearly done more for their pupils. They have made more of a difference to their lives and hence their opportunities after leaving the school, to enhance their 'social mobility'.

Social mobility is a measure of an individual's ability to overcome the disadvantages of their personal background – whether a poor child from a broken home in a high unemployment area of our country can nevertheless rise to the top in terms of educational achievement, earning power and contribution to the leadership of all areas of the nation's future. Many State Boarding schools are very proud of their high 'value added' scores.

Sadly, there still remains overwhelming evidence to show that social mobility has stalled in this country. The Independent schools continue to dominate admissions to the best universities, membership of the leadership of law, journalism, and the military in the UK. As admission to these schools is mostly limited to those whose parents can pay £15,000 to £30,000 per year out of taxed income, they remain well beyond the reach of most families. Only about 7% of all UK children attend HMC schools, and yet the report of the Social Mobility and Child Poverty Commission shows that 71% of senior judges, 62% of senior officers in the armed forces, 55% of Permanent Secretaries, 44% of those on the Sunday Times Rich list and about half of leading TV, film and music professionals all come from this 7% of our children.

The Sutton Trust has spent over seven years striving to *'increase social mobility through education'*.

'Low social mobility and lack of educational opportunity is arguably the biggest social challenge of our times: the income gap between the richest and poorest in society continues to widen, while education opportunities remain overwhelmingly dominated by children from the most privileged homes...........Five elite schools sent more pupils to Oxford and Cambridge universities than nearly 2,000 schools, which make up two thirds of the entire State sector.'

The Sutton Trust has shown that social mobility has declined since the 1950s and that, alongside the United States, Britain now has the lowest level of social mobility of any developed country for which there is data. Some would argue that this was a direct result of the closure of the grammar school system under comprehensive re-organisation, but others would claim that it is much more complicated than that.

My own view is that there is a striking north-south contrast. In England's most northern County, Northumberland, there are now no grammar schools. All secondary pupils attend comprehensive 13-18 High Schools, all of which developed from former grammar schools. They are based in all the historic market towns and major new residential areas, from Hexham in the south to Berwick-on-Tweed in the north. There are also no independent schools outside the Tyneside conurbation apart from one small 3-18 mixed independent school near Berwick with just 256 pupils including just 46 boarders. The last small Prep school near Alnwick closed last year.

Northumberland's strong 13-18 High Schools are supported by the whole local community, rather than just the parents of the most able. They all have large 6th Forms with good A level results which enable young people from every social background to achieve good A level results and gain places at Russell Group universities, including Oxford and Cambridge.

In the 1970s, when Northumberland set up these High schools in all its historic market towns, there were boarding houses for pupils in the Berwick area at Berwick Middle School, at Rothbury Middle School for families living in the Coquet valley and at Haydon Bridge High School. Pupils whose homes lie in the beautiful but remote South Tyne and North Tyne valleys attend Haydon Bridge but during the school week, their home is Ridley Hall, the school's boarding house. This fine listed building is set in beautiful surroundings near to the junction of the South Tyne and

31

Allen rivers. It is just south of Bardon Mill on the edge of the Northumberland National Park.

To be eligible for places at Ridley Hall, students must live in two post code areas which cover the very rural uplands between the North Tyne valley and Otterburn in Redesdale. If they tried to get to school daily, they would have a bus journey of more than ninety minutes so they board at Ridley Hall, a classic case of boarding need.

The Hall is an 18th Century country house once owned by the uncle of the late Queen Mother. When not full of boarders, it also provides a very attractive setting for weekday and weekend courses and conferences for up to sixty resident guests. Set in thirty three acres of grounds and gardens, Ridley Hall is also a wedding venue licensed for civil weddings with a dining room for up to sixty guests. By linking up with the pretty local parish church it has become a popular venue for wedding receptions. School boarding houses are obviously heavily used in school term-time but share with University Halls of residence slack periods when others can make use of them. Some State Boarding schools have grasped the economic opportunity which this presents and, while not becoming boutique hotels in the school holidays, can raise significant income from other uses.

Today, of the three Northumberland boarding houses for pupils attending school from very rural areas, only Ridley Hall has survived. Few State school boarding houses have such a gorgeous setting but all have a need to supplement their income in whatever way they can. With budgets now delegated to schools, boarding houses are run in a much more business-like way than they once were and this must continue if they are to have a future.

~

In contrast, the most southern County on the East Coast, Kent, still has over thirty state grammar schools, including two with boarding places, yet it also has a wealth of independent schools, twenty two of them with boarders. In spite of, or perhaps even because of this heavy dominance of Kent by grammar and independent schools, Kent also has some of the worst performing state secondary schools in the country.

This wealth of successful independent schools is supported by parents with high levels of disposable income either from working in London or from rich families overseas. In London, the dominance of the independent sector is even more marked, again supported by parental wealth inflated at least in part by the escalating house prices in London and the South-East. If your house is valued at £3 million, spending a mere £15,000 - £30,000 a year per child on schooling which is clearly advantageous does not seem to be a great sacrifice. If you live in the most expensive parts of Clapham and Wandsworth, your already expensive house will have increased in price by 19% in the twelve months of 2014. 19% of £1 - £3 million is a cool £190,000 - £380,000, which would fund an awful lot of school fees.

But for most families those £15,000 - £30,000 fees will be impossible. They may aspire to a place for their child at Eton or Harrow but that remains a dream. Even the relatively modest cost of a day place at King's School, Wimbledon, now £19,000 per year, may be beyond most middle class parents as the Head of that school has recently pointed out. He has also said that his school and others face strong competition from state schools which are, in his words, *getting better*.

There is, however, still a perception that most London comprehensive schools are just not good enough for concerned parents to trust their children to. But that is not true of the remaining State Boarding schools. All of them are outside London but more importantly, all are of high quality, achieve good examination results, gain good Ofsted reports and yet are not overtly socially or academically selective.

These SBSA schools are becoming attractive to those independent sector parents looking for a good secondary school. The Head of Thomas', Clapham, an Independent primary school serving relatively affluent parents living 'between the Commons' in what has been called 'nappy valley', advises his parents to continue to spend their money on school fees. But there is a new development. Most of his parents will seek places for their 11 and 13 year old children in the independent sector, boarding and day. But *'have you ever considered,'* asks the Thomas' Head, *'a place at a State Boarding School?'* He asks the question while appearing on a recent SBSA video promoting State Boarding.

If there were more State Boarding school places available in strong comprehensive schools in parts of the country where there are now very few, it would significantly enhance opportunities for social mobility. Such schools have demonstrated that by their academic success that grammar school are not needed to enhance the opportunities of able but poor children. We should leave the debate about a return to grammar school provision across England to the 1960s and focus our efforts on enhancing social mobility for all children disadvantaged by poverty.

3. Boarding Need

There are two main historical reasons why boarding provision developed at schools like Ripon Grammar School. Firstly, such places enabled the Headmaster to enhance his personal income. Secondly, pupils were able to attend from families who were living further than could be easily covered on horseback into school each day. Both were a matter of choice. But there have always been pupils whose parents needed to find a school with such boarding provision because their employment prevented their children to attend school daily.

Serving members of the Armed Forces are subject to frequent postings, some of which are overseas. This inevitably has a disruptive impact on their children's schooling. Similarly, those who serve as diplomats frequently do so in overseas embassies where the local provision of schooling may not provide their children with an appropriate education for entry into Higher Education and careers in the United Kingdom. Thirdly there are many employees of companies who are required to spend time abroad, either leaving their children in boarding places in the United Kingdom or taking them abroad with them and trying to find appropriate local provision.

All three groups of employees are frequently offered financial support for boarding places in United Kingdom schools, in recognition of their children's boarding need. For officers in the Royal Air Force, who are generally posted as individuals, frequent short-term postings at home or abroad creates a real problem of multiple schools for children if families want to move together. In the Army, where whole units move to a new posting together, there is still the need for continuity of education as postings are increasingly short-term. For Royal Navy personnel, the pattern has been for the family to become established in an area near to the base port such as Portsmouth. Children can then enjoy stability of education while the serving father or mother completes tours of duty at sea, thus reducing the boarding need for the children of Navy familes.

The Ministry of Defence recognises this boarding need by providing Continuity of Education Allowances (CEA) for serving military personnel irrespective of rank. The current rate for secondary pupils is £20,007 per year. The majority of claimants of the CEA have traditionally been serving commissioned officers who have a strong tradition of using independent boarding education. This is one reason why the CEA is set at more than twice the cost of boarding at most State Boarding schools. Under the rules of claiming CEA, parents have to pay 10% of the fees which the school charges them. For many serving non-commissioned airmen, this is a real disincentive as their family income may not be sufficient to cover even 10% of the cost of an independent school boarding place.

In 2013/4, the most recent year available, the Ministry of Defence spent £111 million on CEA grants, of which over three quarters were to personnel serving in the United Kingdom but still subject to frequent posting. There are still about 5,000 children of parents in the Armed Forces in boarding places supported by the CEA, mostly at independent schools, although the numbers are declining as the Army and Royal Air Force shrink.

The Foreign Office has a similar scheme for Diplomatic Service personnel who are posted overseas. In 2013/4, this amounted to about £15 million for about 456 staff, again with over 50% actually living in the UK although subject to overseas postings. As they too have traditionally chosen to use independent boarding schools, the grant support available is linked to the level of fees in that sector. It is also claimed that the State Boarding sector is now too small for there to be sufficient places available for both MoD and Foreign Office personnel's children with a reasonable degree of parental choice of school.

But as numbers of claimants decline and availability of places grows, this may not be true for much longer. If more places in State Boarding schools were available and they were better supported by MoD and Foreign Office parents, both Government departments would be able to save significant funds without compromising either the Forces Covenant or the needs of the Diplomatic Service. The MoD is already actively supporting State Boarding by requiring all new CEA applications to include at least one SBSA school.

With the large Army presence at Catterick Garrison to the north and active RAF stations not very far away, a school like Ripon Grammar School is well placed to be attractive to a large number of Ministry of Defence personnel particularly those who would prefer their children to be weekly boarders. However, according to the evidence recently provided by Boarding Schools Association to the House of Commons Defence Select Committee on the Armed Forces Covenant in Action, there were in 2013 no recipients of CEA at Ripon Grammar School and none at any of the other eight state grammar schools with boarding places.

In other words, high quality boarding places for Armed Forces Personnel exist in nine state grammar schools, places which parents nationally are clamouring to access. But as yet they are not being taken up even though the funding for such boarding places is available to such parents and at a cost which would make a significant saving in the Defence Budget. Of course not all the children eligible for CEA would pass the selection tests used by SBSA's nine grammar schools, but many would. Many children receiving CEA support currently pass the selection tests used by selective independent boarding schools.

~

The most significant published research to date on boarding need was by the Cambridge Sociologist, Royston Lambert. In 1966, he carried out a major study which he published as a report '*The State and Boarding Education*'. His findings were used to inform the 1966 and 1968 Newsom Reports. It also concentrated minds in both independent and state boarding.

English Local Authorities had been required under the 1944 Education Act to '*have regard to the expediency of securing the provision of boarding accommodation for pupils for whom education as boarders is considered by their parents and by the authority to be desirable*'. Lambert's study focused on the provision of Local Authority boarding education for normal children, that is, children who did not go to '*special schools for the deaf, handicapped, delicate, maladjusted and others*'.

He found that the definition of boarding need used by different Local Authorities varied so widely that parents in similar circumstances had nothing like an equal chance of help wherever they lived. Given this lack of consistency, there was a need for a national policy which Local Authorities could follow. He also found that what financial help there was for parents was focused on the 'middle-income' sections of the community with the needs of the 'lower-income' groups being largely neglected. This led him to conclude that there were probably at least 48,000 children who needed boarding at that time in England of whom 30,000 were not getting it.

Lambert looked at the criteria which Local Authorities were using to identify 'boarding need', and identified four main categories. Firstly, there were those children who would benefit from living away from home. This included children who were in the care of one parent who was a widow, widower, divorced, separated or deserted. It also included those whose parents though together were too ill or too old to provide adequate care and companionship and those children with severely strained relations with their parents or their siblings. Finally, those children who already had a sibling in boarding school and who want to join them were considered to have a 'need'.

He next considered those children who lacked a stable environment for their full development. This included all children whose education lacked continuity because of parental employment for whatever reason, including service in the Armed Forces or Diplomatic Service, and even those children whose parents were out at work for most of the day for at least five days a week – as a Socialist, Lambert was particularly interested in the provision of weekly boarding for such children which had been set up in the Soviet Union.

Thirdly, for some children the circumstances of their home or neighbourhood prejudiced their chance of fully benefiting from their education or from developing fully. This included children who would have to travel too far to school daily and children in very rural areas where lack of other children prevented the child from having friends of his or her own age. There were also those whose home had been declared unfit for human habitation and those over eleven

39

where siblings over eleven had to share a bedroom. Having nowhere to do school work at home could also be considered as a 'boarding need' by some Authorities.

Lastly, there were those children who would best profit by removal from their present school to a boarding school. This was most commonly related to very individual needs, e.g. the lack of an appropriate course such as a 6th form course in rural areas, or the need to remove the child from particularly damaging local circumstances – such as a destructive local youth culture, could be considered.

Looking back on these 'boarding need' criteria from the vantage point of fifty years later, it is striking how social changes have overwhelmed some of them. Today only 69% of children share their home with both parents. In Royston's day it was 90%. Today, 90% of fathers with dependent children are working and 70% of mothers are working. Today therefore, neither, '*sharing a home with just one parent*', nor '*both parents working*' can be sensible indicators of '*boarding need*'. If they were, hundreds of thousands, if not millions, of children would have such a need.

But many of his criteria do still apply. Parental sickness or disability or old age can still have a huge impact on a child's education. The need for continuity of education is still a clear need, shared by those whose parents are in employment requiring frequent moves and those who follow a way of life which is similarly disruptive of schooling, such as membership of a traveller community. Distance from home to school is still a major problem in very rural areas but it would be difficult to argue the case for rural isolation today, given access by most children to television, tablet 'phones, 'skype', 'face-time', 'twitter' and other social media.

Many secondary schools now recognise the need for some children to do their homework at school with organised after-school homework clubs, so it would be difficult to argue for this to be a clear '*boarding need*' today. Particular academic needs can still lead to a 'boarding need'. For some 16-19 students this can be met by hostel arrangements which are much less controlling than traditional boarding school houses. Nevertheless, parents may still prefer their sons or daughters to be in the more secure school environment.

The need to remove the child from damaging circumstances is still a major source of '*boarding need*' and this can cover a wide range of circumstances. The girl whose mother earns her living from men on the sea-front of a run-down coastal town or in a city red-light district would be a strong case for a boarding place where she is free from the harassment of her mother's customers. The boy whose parents have gone through a messy divorce and who fight over which of them should provide a stable home situation would be better at least for the working week away from the conflicts of home.

Some Local Authorities, notably Norfolk and Essex had Social Service departments which were actively involved in supporting young people in boarding places. Norfolk paid for over a hundred such cases of 'boarding need' in just one large state secondary boarding school in the 1980s and 1990s. But the anti-boarding culture which developed in many Local Authority Social Service Departments led many to oppose supporting cases of 'boarding need'. Many social workers were deeply suspicious of boarding schools in general and many still are.

More recently, as Local Authorities have faced increasingly damaging cuts in their finances, it has become more and more difficult to justify spending scarce public money on supporting children in boarding placements. By 2005, across the whole UK there were only fifty children in boarding places funded by Local Authorities. The role has been handed over to charities such as the Buttle Trust and the Royal National Children's Foundation (RNCF) which still provides financial and professional support for many children with a boarding need.

Today, the majority of 'children in need' as defined by the Children's Act 1989 will continue to be taken into care. In 2013, there were just under 70,000 of them aged from 5 to 17 with 75% in a foster placement and 25% cared for in Local Authority Children's Homes. Unless some dramatic improvements can be brought about, these 'looked after' children will continue to have very poor educational outcomes, be twice as likely to be permanently excluded from school and have four times the national average rate of involvement with the Police and Courts. There is now a real imperative to seek new solutions to meeting such children's needs and a growing conviction that boarding schools in the state sector could provide at least part of the answer.

4. Boarding House

The boys' boarding house in which I spent much of my
secondary education

In England's state sector, there are only a handful of schools
which are 'traditional boarding schools' i.e. schools which are
set up to cater for the needs of a majority of boarders.
Brymore and Sexey's in Somerset, Wymondham in Norfolk,
and Old Swinford in the West Midlands are all schools with
a majority, or near majority of boarders, but they also have
day and day-boarding pupils. Two schools with links to the
military, Welbeck College and the Duke of York's Royal
Military Academy are both full boarding schools with no day
pupils. Five other schools, Cranbrook in Kent, Gordon's in

Surrey, Hockerill in Hertfordshire, Holyport in Berkshire and the Royal Albert and Alexandra also in Surrey have between 25% and 45% boarders.

Boarding places in the great majority of State Boarding schools are very different. Their boarders are a minority part of large day schools, commonly about 10% or less of the total pupil roll, living in one or more boarding houses. Such houses have their strengths – boarders can get to know a small and secure community of their peers away from the pressures of a large school in an atmosphere which can be more like a family. They also have the weakness that the boarders' needs can get overlooked as the leadership of the school has to focus on provision for the day pupil majority.

But, in terms of their survival over the last fifty years, such minority boarding schools have shown an extraordinary resilience. Of the State Boarding schools which had this low proportion of boarders fifty years ago, just under half still exist and still have boarders today, twenty four schools. This number is actually now growing with the opening or re-opening of five houses in what are mainly day schools.

In contrast, schools which have a high proportion or a majority of boarders have actually declined by over 75%. Some have closed altogether, including the boarding secondary modern schools which closed at the time of secondary comprehensive re-organisation. Others have lost all their boarders because the Local Authority or the Governors or the Head no longer saw a need to provide for boarders.

~

When I became involved in running such boarding houses and in leading state schools with both a minority and a majority of boarding, it was often helpful to think back to

44

my own experience as a pupil. I boarded for six years in just such a 'minority' boarding house', a community of about thirty boarding boys which was part of a very large and very successful independent London boys' day school.

My parents did not want me to attend my father's independent school in London and yet wanted me to go to the best school they could afford, just as parents today want the best for their children. They sent me as a weekly boarder to a highly selective and independent boys' school in West London. They would have to pay the boarding fee, as do most of the parents of boarders in state schools today, but I managed to win a bursary which covered most of the day fees. According to my mother, it was too far to travel daily from our house in Bickley, Kent, to the school they chose.

'Anyway,' she said, 'boarding would do you good'.

My highly competitive independent school gave me an excellent academic education and useful boarding survival strategies. Our home from Monday morning to Friday after school was School House but it was really little more than a hostel. The 'day-room' at street level consisted of a large space of working tables and hard chairs surrounded by lockers. It became our 'prep room' every weekday evening. In the corner a much smaller room provided the small team of 6th Form Prefects with some privacy. Senior, middle and junior dormitories were piled above each other to complete a five layered slab cake of a building which sat alongside the busy trunk road leading out of London. Just across a side road, the fine brick buildings of the day school housed eight hundred day pupils. School House had neither grandeur nor architectural style.

It had been built about seventy years before as a classroom block for juniors and became a boarding house when the youngest boys moved to new buildings. Our House was still as functional as a pile of classrooms – except that there were now beds where once there were desks. An attached wing housed the staff, our bachelor housemaster and a couple who served as matron and duty master. On the top floor, a small flat was home to the resident house tutor who was also a music master at the school. Along the sunny side of the House, the traffic thundered past. On the sunless north side, a concrete yard served as our exercise space. It had a block of outside toilets in the corner, a row of cubicles shielded by a brick wall.

This wall was important to us boarders providing what little in-house exercise and entertainment we had. It returned our footballs in winter and our tennis balls in summer, as we kicked and thwacked away our boredom in the spare minutes between coming back from school and the time for 'tea'. The residents of the block of flats which overlooked our yard must have heaved a sigh of relief when the monotonous thud of ball on brick ceased when the tea-bell rang. After a quick re-fuelling of mind and body, we settled down for the hours of 'prep' which filled every evening, until we were sent up to bed

The brick wall also shielded the row of outside lavatories which served all the boarders during the day when access to dormitories and upstairs bathrooms was denied us. Many schools had outside toilets in those days, where boys could enjoy their scatological activities without polluting the air breathed by teachers. The inner side of the wall formed a basic urinal with a horizontal pipe and a gutter, regularly blocked with falling leaves and frozen in winter.

Life in School House was Spartan but relatively undemanding. Mornings were brisk and busy. In the winter,

46

with no heating in the dormitory, it was just a quick leap out of a warm bed to wash and get downstairs for breakfast. The hoar frost on the inside of the windows of our muggy dormitory would be gone by the time we left the house for school, together with the rude messages to the flats. When we came back after school, there was little time to get into real trouble. Television in homes had only just been developed and had not yet reached School House. In the late 1950s according to Philip Larkin, sexual intercourse had not yet started. As it was an all boys' house in an all boys' school there was little opportunity for the latter, except for the odd experimental fumble between consenting boys behind the shed in the school's Biology Garden.

Being a boarder during the school week taught me how to cope with minor assaults such as a carefully aimed knuckle punch from bigger boys while we queued for tea. These always produced a 'dead arm' until the nerve came back to life again. Such events were then accepted as part of boarding school life. Now, they would be described as bullying. Once, the occupants of the next two beds in the Junior Dormitory wondered if it was possible to fit a boarder into one of our school trunks we had just unpacked. They chose me and it was.

After a brief scuffle, they closed the lid, swung the hasp across the staple and went down to tea. The trunk was not airtight so I survived, if a bit hungry, and after tea I was released. It seemed that no-one had noticed my enforced absence from the dining room. The level of supervision by staff was minimal – mostly it was the Prefects who kept an eye on us. Only during 'Prep' were we supervised by adults presumably to prevent us from sharing each other's efforts.

~

47

Boarding houses today are much better regulated and such cavalier attitudes to Health and Safety and to the care of children have quite rightly long since gone from schools. But it is useful for those who run Houses and Schools to be able to remember what it was like to be a boarder, just how bored we were for much of the time and just how powerless. We knew we were pawns in a system which told our parents that it had our best interest at heart. It often seemed at the time utterly unconcerned about the realities of boarding house life.

We were fed three meals a day and encouraged to sleep at night. We were more or less free from extremes of hot and cold and kept dry. We received a superb academic education which would open doors which many of us would never had been able to enter without the advantage of attending such a school. But it was a grey environment in which to spend one's adolescence, although the lack of any sort of visual beauty in the House was of little concern to most of us. Thirteen year old boys are generally not much interested in pictures unless they are of well-endowed and thinly veiled girls, but there were those boys who longed for some of the softness and colour of their own homes.

We had no garden, no interesting pictures on walls, no female company except the well-starched lady who claimed to be our Matron. She seemed to lack both sympathy and nursing expertise. The one area where we had a rich diet of culture was the monthly visit for the more senior boys to an opera or a Shakespeare play in one of the theatres of London's West End. Escaping for an evening to sit in the 'gods' and watch Eugene Onegin or the Merchant of Venice, and then to have the opportunity to discuss what we

48

remembered with the master who had taken us, was a real enrichment of our education.

~

In the 1960s, the old historic County of Lincolnshire had eight schools with boarding houses, two in the City of Lincoln and six spread across the market towns of Brigg, Caistor, Market Rasen, Louth, Grantham and Stamford. This wealth of state boarding provision was in part a reflection of the strong presence of the RAF in the County together with the very rural nature of much of it. Over the years, and with the decline of the number of RAF stations, most of these school boarding houses have closed but at De Aston School in Market Rasen, boarding has continued. The school is now a large mixed comprehensive serving the town and surrounding rural area. Boarding started in Market Rasen over a century ago when the attics of the old boys' grammar school Head's house were used for boarders. Thanks to stable and expert staffing, support from a succession of Heads and a vigorous approach to recruiting boarders, the boarding house, still occupying most of the old Head's House, has flourished. Ofsted rates De Aston boarding provision as 'outstanding'.

Another helpful feature of Market Rasen is that it is still has a train service. Parents living in London may be unhappy with the quality of their local schooling. London families are increasingly interested in sending their children as weekly boarders to a school which takes boys and girls, of all abilities, from 11 to 18. De Aston meets all three requirements, has good rail links to London and is affordable by many earning London salaries.

It has also developed a strong link with families in Spain, particularly those in Madrid and Valencia who have a

49

business interest in tourism. One member of the family, usually a son, may be sent to board in England for the equivalent of their Y9 year, Having honed their colloquial English skills to a good level, such Spanish pupils then return to Spain to complete Years 10 and 11, only to reappear in England for the two year Business Studies 6th Form course which De Aston offers.

~

There was no tradition of school boarding in Skegness although the sea-side town had very many boarding houses for holiday makers! For some Heads and Governors, having a boarding house was seen as a mark of quality. Good schools had them. The Head of Skegness Grammar School persuaded his governors and the County Council in 1991 that if Louth, Grantham and Caistor had boarding, so should Skegness. At the same time, a County Council old people's home in the small town of Wainfleet about five miles south of Skegness was closing and the school re-opened it as a boarding house. For many years, boarders travelled each day by train to and fro between Wainfleet and Skegness.

The school celebrates this separation of school and house as a clear advantage. In the words of John and Helen Nuttall, current House-parents: *'Having this clear divide between where a child goes to lessons and where they can relax and focus on developing other interests and hobbies sets us apart from most of our peers. It essentially means we offer all the advantages of a traditional academic boarding house, but also all the comforts of a warm home environment. We can say this with first-hand experience because we also call Wainfleet Hall home. When we became house parents in 2012, we moved into the building with our own children. We have seen how much they have grown from spending time with the culturally diverse group of students who stay with us, and we do everything we can to ensure this sense of being part of a community is the most valued part of life here with us.'*

The Hall really is the Nuttall's home as they have let their own property. Their sons have grown up with the boarders and enjoy friendships with boarders across the world, including holiday visits to Spain and the Far East. Helen's interest in gardening and things environmental has produced a 'Hall pond', dug out and nurtured with the boarders' help. Their son's chickens range freely across the Hall grounds and their care is shared with the boarders.

One frustration is that Ofsted, in their concern for child-protection, questioned the daily train journeys between Skegness and Wainfleet as boarders had to walk from school to station in Skegness and a few hundred yards from station to Hall in Wainfleet. The fact is that hundreds of other Skegness school-children walk to school across the town unescorted every day. At the beginning and end of every term, the Wainfleet Hall boarders travel on their own via flights and trains thousands of miles from home in Madrid or Macau to Wainfleet Hall. Both facts were in Ofsted's view irrelevant. During the school week, boarders could not travel anywhere without staff supervision, so the boarding house now has two minibuses to take boarders to and from school.

As well as having an unusual arrangement for housing boarders five miles from the day school, Skegness Grammar School is the only boarding school in the State sector to date which has become a part of a sponsored academy chain. The David Ross Education Trust (DRET), set up by the millionaire founder of Carphone Warehouse, now sponsors over twenty primary, secondary and special schools in the East Midlands. David Ross's grandfather owned one of Grimsby's largest fishing fleet and founded Ross Foods which became Ross Frozen Foods. David was a boarder at Uppingham School and has based the philosophy of his Academy chain on the famous Head of Uppingham, Edward Thring's, belief that '*every child can do something well*'. Support for boarding at Skegness Grammar School has been one benefit from this academy sponsorship link. When it became widely known that most State Boarding schools were in desperate need of cash for maintaining the fabric of their Houses, the DRET provided a grant of £0.25 million for the renovation of Wainfleet Hall. Another feature of this support is the 'boarding scholarship' scheme which offers financial support for 6th Form students from any of the DRET schools to do their A levels at Skegness Grammar School and board at Wainfleet Hall. This enables young people from some of the poorest areas of the East Midlands to access 6th Form education, another very good example of State Boarding being used to enhance social mobility.

~

In Stamford, Lincolnshire, the Endowed Schools still maintain boarding houses for boys and for girls, but they are both now in the independent sector. In the City of Lincoln, although boarding ceased at the City schools thirty years ago, a new boarding house for 6th form students opened at the Priory LSST School in 2012. This highly successful state school has now become an Academy and the lead school of its own Academy federation. The Robert de Cheney boarding house on the Priory LSST site provides sixty boarding places in a brand new boarding house funded partly by a capital grant from the Department for Education. The bid for this grant referred to the school's strategic position in Lincoln, not far from RAF Waddington and well placed to offer places to Ministry of Defence boarders. Other 6th form applicants have to have UK or EU passports or the right of residence in the UK, but can come from anywhere in the world. The first boarders moved in in 2012 and the boarding option is proving attractive to 6th Formers joining both the Priory LSST and the other federated Academies.

~

The challenge of securing funding to maintain and enhance facilities in relatively small boarding houses remains a major concern. Those with charitable foundations which own property or funds can make good use of their assets. Those without can struggle without funding from National or Local Government. National Government has supported State Boarding strongly with capital grants in recent years. A total of £25 million was allocated in 2005-6 and shared between four SBSA schools, Brymore School, Lancaster Royal Grammar School, Wymondham College and Old Swinford Hospital. A further four schools, Steyning Grammar School, Shaftesbury School, the Royal Alexandra and Albert School and Hockerill Anglo-European College, received grants from an allocation of £16 million in 2008-2010.

These major grants ensured an overall increase in the number of state boarding places but some SBSA schools have struggled to ensure that their boarding survives. Boarding provision in majority day state schools will always be a very low priority for local funding as the priority will always be provision for local children from the area which is the school's principal focus. Funding primarily for children who come as boarders and are not part of the local community will always be difficult to justify, unless funding from new sources can be secured.

Two other boarding houses attached to large day schools in rural areas are also interesting, those at Wem in Shropshire and at Crediton in Devon. Both towns have had houses for boy boarders since the founding of the boys' grammar schools in the 17th Century. Both are now large, flourishing, comprehensive schools and both still celebrate their boarding provision. The Thomas Adam School, College and House in Wem now has over 1200 pupils, boys and girls, from 11 to 18. Adams House provides boarding places for up to 65 boarders and the school celebrates the fact that, although they must all have UK or EU passports, they come from all over the world. For young people in a quiet corner of rural England to have the opportunity to live in a multicultural society and to learn to respect and value each other is a powerful experience. They would not have that opportunity if boarders with homes in the USA, Uganda, Kuwait, UAE, Hong Kong, Germany, France, Greece, Spain & Nigeria were not able to join them.

In my own small boarding house in London in the 1950s, we shared life with boys from Thailand, France and Germany and we were the richer for it. When Sir Thomas Adams founded the Free School of Wem in 1650 he was a leading member of the Drapers Company of the City of London. Like other City Companies, the Drapers were linked into a developing international trading network exploiting not just the English market but new opportunities established by English traders all over the then known world. He would have approved of the international nature of Adams House, named in his honour.

QE Academy Trust serves the town of Crediton in Devon and the surrounding area. This school has gone through a similar series of mutations from boys' grammar school through comprehensive reorganisation and now into an academy with a very strong community role. Through each change, the school has retained a commitment to boarding.

They currently have fifty boarding places. If all these places are filled, they generate a small surplus on the boarding account. Crediton's boarders are largely in the Sixth Form, with several Hong Kong residents and some German students who come for a year or even shorter. These boarders do put additional demands on the main school, but they also greatly enrich it. As in all State Boarding schools, boarding has to be self-financing from boarding fees. If boarding numbers fall, there are few savings to be had from staffing because the numbers are already relatively small. But the cost of any staff redundancies would have to be borne by the Academy Trust so there is a real incentive to maintain the boarding numbers or even better to expand boarding for example to 75.

In Crediton's case, the school still occupies two main teaching sites with boys' boarding in a large, old and expensive house on a third site. This boarding house and the land it occupies is a significant asset held by the Governors. It could be sold off and the capital raised could then be used to construct a purpose built boarding house on the land behind the School Sports Hall. This would allow for growth in boarding numbers at a time of falling rolls in the main school, help assure the financial sustainability of the boarding facility and significantly reduce running costs.

However, the capital raised could alternatively be used solely to enhance day provision and end boarding. This would incur inevitable redundancies costs falling on the school. There is also the highly emotive issue of the ending of a boarding tradition which in Crediton's case goes back over four hundred years. As QEAT is now the sole remaining state boarding opportunity in the whole of Devon and Cornwall, the whole region would have no State Boarding asset within a reasonable travelling distance for families. Such decisions are very difficult for schools, but, at least, the future is now in principle in their own hands rather than in a decision making process by politicians and administrators at County Hall. That was what brought about the closure of many of the State Boarding schools and boarding houses between the 1950s and 1990s. Almost two thousand State Boarding places were lost over these years as Local Authorities closed eleven small boarding schools.

~

One Northern comprehensive State Boarding school which is flourishing is Keswick School, older than Cambridge University and re-founded in the 19th C by the same Victorian educational pioneer who founded St George's School in Harpenden, another very successful SBSA school. The town of Keswick in Cumbria sits in the heart of the most glorious Lake District scenery, with Skiddaw, England's fourth highest mountain behind the town and Derwentwater to the South. The setting for the school is just one of the superlative things about it. It is Outstanding according to Ofsted, with excellent results at GCSE and A level, yet it is a comprehensive offering a huge range of educational and cultural opportunities to boys and girls from the town and from a wide swathe of Cumbria, right across to the West Cumbrian towns of Whitehaven and Workington. Now an Academy, effectively an independent state school, the current Head relishes the freedom which this gives. 'We plough our own furrow here!'

Keswick School has used inclusion in the 'Good Schools Guide' to promote itself as *'one of the best comprehensives in the Country'*. Ninety per cent of year 13 leavers go on to university, including a handful each year to Oxbridge (five offers in 2014), and 10 per cent of leavers go on to study at university abroad.

In a school of over one thousand pupils, there are just 54 boarding places in a boarding house on the main school site. This too has been judged 'outstanding' by Ofsted and the school could fill three times as many places if there was room to expand. Lack of capital funding and shortage of space are frustrating this ambition but State Boarding at Keswick School remains strong. What started many years ago as an obvious answer to the problem of getting to school from homes beyond a day's ride on a horse now offers modern boarding to students who may well fly in from all over Europe and beyond.

5.   Boarding Schools as charities

Constant Lambert in his Christ's Hospital uniform in
1917

It is interesting to speculate whether Thomas Cromwell, of
Wolf Hall fame, or Thomas Arnold, the Head of Rugby
School at the time in which 'Tom Brown's Schooldays' was
set, had the greater influence on England's boarding schools.
Arnold turned a small boys' school which was little better
than a battle-field when he came into a very successful
boarding school, a model which has been copied all over the
English-speaking world. But perhaps Cromwell has the
stronger claim.

Cromwell was Henry VIII's agent for the closure of the
monasteries, transferring their assets from the Church to the

King, who promptly gave or sold them to his supporters. Many of our great independent boarding schools were founded from the estates and the finances of these monasteries; King's Canterbury is a good example. Some like Charterhouse were founded in the ruins of monastic buildings when rich benefactors bought the properties and set up schools as a charitable provision of education for the poor. Thomas Cromwell could therefore be seen as the 'god-father' of many famous schools, although there was nothing very 'godly' about the process. Having been founded as charities because they provided education when the church ceased to do so, these schools have been regarded as charities ever since.

I have never worked in one of England's great boarding Public schools. Charterhouse, Eton, Harrow, Rugby, Shrewsbury, Westminster, and Winchester were the seven included in the Public Schools Act of 1868 and confirmed as being free from any Crown, Church or Government control. They continued to be truly 'independent'. Two more schools, St Paul's and Merchant Taylors were both day schools and already independent by their own statutes, so these nine schools became *certain Public Schools* under the Act.

Many other schools followed, until the term 'public school' came to refer to boys 13-18 schools which were mainly boarding, charged high fees and had an element of social exclusivity. Many of them had originally been founded as charities. But there were other large boarding boys' schools which have remained truly charitable institutions, founded to provide education for the sons of the poor and continuing in that role to this day.

~

On a frosty morning in January 1966, I woke to the sound of marching feet. Bleary eyed, I peered through the curtains. In the semi darkness along the road under my window, platoons of boys in blue coats with yellow stockings were marching past. I remembered where I was. Oxford University Education Department had found me a place for my teaching practice term at Christ's Hospital, the boys' boarding school in Sussex. My window looked out from the House Tutor's bedsitting room onto the road that ran through the school. House by house, in column of three with a senior boy at their head, they were marching to breakfast. As the other houses passed my window, the boys of Lamb A and Lamb B, the two semi-detached houses in one building, formed up in the road, set off after them and I went back to sleep.

My term in Lamb B, by far the most useful part of a year's Teacher Training, was a wonderful induction into secondary teaching. The school is and was unique. A full boarding school, with boys selected for entry by their ability at eleven, CH or 'Housey' as it is sometimes known was a true charity. Boys were 'presented' for admission by whoever paid their school fees, be it an individual donor, a City Company, a Charitable Trust or even a Local Authority. There were boys in the school whose places were funded from public money via Local Authority grants – they were truly 'boarding on the State'. Some were children who very much need a stable and secure boarding place, whose home circumstances for whatever reason were preventing them from making progress at day school. They had a 'boarding need'. Most recent Heads of the school have been members of HMC identifying the school as one of the leading boarding independent schools.

When Henry VIII closed the great monastic houses, the property of the Grey Friars in London's Newgate Street was given by the King to the City of London Corporation. They set up Christ's Hospital and, in 1553 the school received a Royal Charter from King Edward VI. From the start it was a school for the orphan children of the poor of London. The same charitable foundation included provision for the sick at St Thomas's Hospital and for 'idle vagabonds' at Bridewell Hospital. From the start both girls and boys were admitted to Christ's Hospital, although the boys always outnumbered the girls. Most of the boys left school at fifteen but those who stayed on were prepared for entry to University at the Grammar School section of the school or for service at sea at the Royal Mathematical School.

When the Great Plague hit London in 1665, Christ's Hospital lost thirty two children. A year later, the Great Fire destroyed almost all of its buildings. In 1682, a new school was built at Hertford north of London, and added to over the centuries to create the magnificent buildings where the school remained until 1902. In that year, all the boys transferred to a new site in the Sussex countryside just outside West Horsham. It even has its own railway station! The girls who had a separate school in Hertfordshire joined the boys on the West Horsham site in 1985. Throughout its history, Christ's Hospital has received generous benefactions, for buildings and for the support of pupils. It is one of the schools in HMC which is both a great boarding Public School and an unchallenged charity. Ever since its founding, Christ's Hospital has provided a first class boarding education for able but needy children who would otherwise have no opportunity to enjoy such a benefit.

Today, all pupils are selected on academic ability and on a means test of parental income which must demonstrate some financial need. Roughly 20% are assessed as having 'high need', 60% 'medium to high need' and 20% 'low' need, but unlike almost all other independent schools, the ability to pay the full cost of a place does not automatically give a parent the opportunity to access a place for their son or daughter.

All the current 820 boarders receive some support from Governors or from a huge range of charitable trusts, from City Companies, Armed Forces Charities and those supporting children from particular parishes, Local Authority areas or communities. Some of these boarders are therefore paid for out of public money, they are literally *'boarding on the state'* although they attend an independent school.

As a young chemistry graduate just starting to learn the craft of the teacher, I could not have had a better induction than that term at Christ's Hospital. The school provided a base for me in Lamb B, where in exchange for evening supervision duties, I received three meals a day and an adequate if not palatial room to live in. The Masters' Common room was the nearest thing to a Gentleman's Club that I have ever experienced. It had leather arm chairs in a vast sitting room, a billiard room complete with a barrel of beer and a large dining room in which we ate delicious three course dinners every day of the week. I first met a ramekin dish at dinner at Christ's Hospital. Every time I am served a tasty starter in such a piece of porcelain, I am reminded of my ten weeks there, learning to teach. Christ's Hospital recognised that without committed and professional teaching staff prepared to do boarding duties, the school could not function. The men and a few women who made up the Masters' Common Room were very well looked after.

~

The twenty Lamb B boys who shared the Junior Dormitory next to my Tutor's Room were noisy, cheerful and full of energy. Their 'blue coat and yellow stockings' uniform, worn with white shirt and tab and heavy black shoes, was all provided by the school. That is still true today, although the houses are now much more comfortable. One of my first tasks in 1966 was to sort out a complaint from the youngest boys who claimed that they could not sleep. Their iron bed-frames had wooden planks on which their mattresses rested. Half of the planks had been 'borrowed' by older boarders. Boys at Christ's Hospital really were 'boarders'! The worst case had just three planks on which to balance his mattress for the night! It was all relatively good natured and eventually the boards were returned so that all could sleep in peace.

'It happened to us too, Sir,' was the only reason offered for this mild form of persecution.

While discipline in school boarding houses was enforced by Prefects, the Housemasters responsible for many Public school boarding houses could actually live in a house detached from the dormitories, a situation which lasted in many independent boarding schools well into the 1970s. But at Christ's Hospital by 1966, all the Houses had resident Housemasters and '*being on duty*' meant not just being in your flat or bed-sitting room but actually being amongst the boarders, fully responsible for pupil behaviour. The role was shared in Christ Hospital and most schools between the Housemaster and one or more House Tutors.

63

This was my role in Lamb B during teaching practice and shortly afterwards I applied for a job at King's School, Worcester, to teach Chemistry and to act as a House Tutor. David Annett was the distinguished Head at the time; an expert at recruiting young teachers to full time teaching posts which turned out, after interview with David, to involve numerous additional roles. I was invited to Worcester. A few hours later, I was pleased to know that I would join his staff to teach chemistry, and also be the Tutor in Castle House, coach the Colts VIII on the river, support the school Scout Troup and even teach Divinity to thirteen year-olds. There was little time left for any other interests I might have had but that first teaching job at King's was an excellent introduction to the role of the schoolmaster!

Being '*on duty*' in Castle House, one of the school's boarding houses facing onto College Green in the shadow of the Cathedral, involved two evenings a week and every other weekend, primarily to give the Housemaster the occasional break. There were about thirty boys in the House, mostly there as fee-paying boarders from the rural areas of Worcestershire, but there were also a few boys from Worcester with a '*boarding need*'.

They had passed the 11+ exam from a City Primary School and been given a fully-funded boarding place. These boys really were '*state school boarders*' as their school place was financed by the Local Authority as part of the Worcester selective system and their boarding place was paid for by the Worcester Social Services Department out of public money. But they were a minority. The King's School, like most Direct Grant Grammar Schools, was full of able children from relatively affluent middle-class homes.

Some of the '*boarding need*' boys came from dysfunctional homes and some had behavioural problems – they were some of the '*odd balls*' of the school. The Head had explained to me the way he allocated boys to houses.

'I put all the odd-balls in Castle – that way they annoy each other and no-one else!'

I enjoyed working with the Castle team of Prefects who knew their job and allowed me to maintain the illusion that I was in charge when on duty. The only potential conflict between us was at Evening Prayers. My efforts to ensure that the occasion was an '*act of worship of a mainly Christian character'* conflicted with their determination to introduce Castle House to Chinese love poems, Hindu mysticism and Quaker silences, just to annoy me. The school found a small flat for me in Edgar Street just next to College Green from which I could do evening duties without actually living in the House.

~

The Labour Government ended the Direct Grant system in 1976, giving the schools involved the option of becoming comprehensive or going independent. The King's School, together with most of the City Grammar Schools, joined the independent sector. Nationally, this had the effect of boosting the academic focus of that sector as it now educated very many very able young people. In many parents' eyes, especially parents whose own schooling had been in state grammar schools, independent schools became the place they wanted their able children to be educated. By 1996, the King's School had also become fully co-educational and by 1999 fully day. As the school history puts it '*a new Bursar and new Headmaster moved King's into the 21st Century*'.

65

The former boarding houses around College Green were used by the school for offices and for teaching. The assumption was that there was simply no need to continue with an out-of-date boarding tradition which had started well before the 1551 Royal Charter. It might survive at Eton and very many other Public Schools, but at King's School, Worcester, it died when the Head and the Governors could no longer see a need to maintain it.

~

The first Newsom Report '*Half our Future*' of 1963 had provided Harold Wilson's Labour Government with the evidence on which to reform grammar and secondary modern schools. Tony Crosland as Wilson's Secretary of State for Education had published his 10/65 Circular 'requesting' Local Authorities to set out their plans for Secondary School Re-Organisation on Comprehensive principles. As capital grant support for school building development was focused on implementing comprehensive schemes, it was effectively a 'requirement'.

Not far behind came the 1968 publication of the Labour Government's second Newsom Report, on the conclusions of the Public Schools Commission. This had been set up to consider ways in which legislation could encourage independent boarding schools, the Public Schools, to become more integrated into the national provision of education.

After years of deliberation, the 1968 Report was published with fifty two recommendations. Many of these have just quietly happened over the last forty eight years without any legislation. The ability range of pupils in many independent boarding schools has increased as the competition for places has eased. In many Public Schools including Eton, family connections which led to children being 'put down' for a school at birth (a strange expression usually applied to suffering animals) have been phased out with entry being focused on actual academic performance at 13.

Very many independent schools do now work closely with maintained schools – some, including Wellington and Eton, have actually sponsored state boarding schools as Academies. Independent schools wishing to join the maintained sector have done so –again as Academies, with Liverpool College and Polam Hall both now state funded.

More co-educational boarding schools have developed from all boys schools – sometimes in competition for girls with neighbouring all girls' schools as has happened in York. The ending of discrimination against immigrant children was recommended. The Chairman of HMC has recently pointed out that *'independent schools across the UK now more ethnically diverse than their state-maintained counterparts'*.

All these changes were recommended by Newsom's 1968 report. Its authors also supported public expenditure on boarding education being based solely on need. They estimated that *'80,000 children in England and Wales would require boarding places by 1980, 45,000 of which should be found in an integrated system of state and independent boarding schools'* but the Report was never implemented.

Not all the members of the Commission agreed with the Report. The two independent school Heads and the Director General of the CBI who served as members all refused to sign it. John Vaisey, the academic economist with a particular interest in education, insisted that the report should include his 'note of dissention', with the memorable comment:

'The main objection to private schools is that they are socially divisive. Some of them happen to have beds. It therefore seems less revolutionary to change the bodies in the beds than to eliminate the beds. It is as though Henry VIII had not dismantled the monasteries, but filled them with social need cases, after an exhaustive social survey of the number of people in the population who felt the urge for a life of contemplation in a cell. There is a degree of confusion in attempting to "solve" a social question by throwing out the middle class and replacing it by a different social group.'

The Report was in any case overtaken by events. Patrick Gordon-Walker, Crosland's successor as Labour Secretary of State for Education only served for nine months before being replaced by Edward Short. By 1970, no further action on the proposals to integrate the Public Schools had taken place when Margaret Thatcher was put in charge of Education in Ted Heath's Conservative government. The Independent schools, boarding and day, remained largely unchanged and were allowed to evolve at their own pace. But there was one recommendation from 1968 which lingered on in Labour Party ambitions:

'the fiscal reliefs of schools which are charities but do not serve a truly charitable purpose should be ended'.

In other words, the tax benefits which independent schools all enjoyed because they were classified as charities should be challenged and, if possible, ended. When in 2006, the Labour Government passed the Charities Act, Dame Suzi Leather, a strong Labour Party supporter, was appointed to chair the Charities Commission.

The Commission took the view that the *'advancement of education'* could no longer be one of the *'charitable purposes'* for which charities could be established, unless the charity could demonstrate a *'public benefit'*. It was this test that independent

68

schools had to meet if they wished to continue to enjoy the tax advantages of charitable status.

Just to *provide education* was not considered a charitable purpose, although it had been since the Charitable Uses Act of 1602. The Charity Commission's new definition meant that if a school *provided education* in exchange for an economic fee, it could not claim to be doing so for a *public benefit* but only for a private one, for the parents of the pupils at the school. If the school offered bursaries or provided teaching or coaching for free for children from the local area, then a fee-paying school could demonstrate *public benefit* and therefore claim to be a charity.

In July 2009, the Charity Commission investigated five private schools in the North West of England against this definition of *public benefit* and concluded that two of them gave insufficient benefit to the public and had therefore failed the proposed test. These schools were told that they would lose their charitable status unless they gave more bursaries and both complied, keeping their status as charities.

The Independent Schools Council on behalf of all independent schools in membership of the major Associations decided to challenge the *public benefit* test as now defined by the Charity Commission at a tribunal. The Charity Commission lost, having spent £185,000 in legal fees. It was accused of exceeding its powers and giving undue weight to the Labour Party's views in its guidance to schools.

Even so, from that time onwards, the information provided by Independent schools and their Associations has laid great stress, not just on their academic excellence but also on the generosity with which they now offer bursaries, give access to their facilities and share some of their teaching. Their schools were founded as charities, in most cases hundreds of years ago, and are keen to demonstrate that they still have a charitable role today.

Christ's Hospital has always been accepted as a major national charity, by all Political Parties in Government and in Opposition. Eton College, Rugby School, Uppingham School and many others all started as charitable foundations with a national or local role and all developed into major Public Schools. All continue to claim charitable status for tax purposes and all have retained a commitment to boarding and independence from any State control.

But there are schools which have very similar national or local charitable roots which have remained within the state sector. In the West Midlands town of Stourbridge, near to the ancient parish church of Old Swinford, a boarding school for boys was founded by Thomas Foley. He was a 17th century ironmaster and landowner, who use his wealth to provide an education for '*sixty poor but honest boys*', in what was once known as Foley's Bluecoat School. The boys were to be nominated by specific parishes in the three counties which meet near Stourbridge, Worcestershire, Staffordshire and Warwickshire. Foley's school became better known as Old Swinford Hospital. It has served the Stourbridge community and the wider West Midlands since 1667.

In his will, Foley entrusted the school to a group of men, known as Feoffees, which have always included one of his descendants, starting with his son. They are still involved with the school today. There are still Stourbridge boys offered places at the school although the majority of boys come from much further afield as the school is still predominately a boarding school. It still occupies the original site in the Old Swinford part of Stourbridge and has established a very strong reputation for academic success, rugby football and the quality of its boarding provision. Up to 1950, it continued to be a charity school, but then became a Voluntary Aided School with the Feoffees owning the property and having a majority on the Governing Body. Today it is an 11-18 comprehensive school with over four hundred boarding places for boys, which also admits boys at 11 as day pupils and day girls into the very large sixth form.

As Andrew Adonis has written, 'strong leadership is crucial to the success of a school'. Old Swinford Hospital has benefitted enormously from having three very strong Headmasters since 1978, Chris Potter, Melvyn Roffe and Peter Jones. Chris was the longest serving, from 1978 to 2001, a period which included the move to Grant Maintained status away from control by Dudley Local Authority. I knew Chris well as a fellow State Boarding school Head and admired his ability to raise standards in his school and to persuade grant-giving bodies to fund the building of new boarding houses. Chris was awarded the OBE for his work in leading the school at a time of rapid development. The school has returned the honour by naming the newest and largest boarding house, Potter House.

Melvyn Roffe took over in 2001 and developed the school further, most notably by encouraging the development of a Business Studies specialism at a time when national government was encouraging secondary schools to develop a particular curriculum focus. From 2004, the school became a Business and Enterprise Specialist School and was very successful at attracting business sponsorship. In 2006, the new business centre, the 'Business Hub', was opened by the Director General of the Institute of Directors. It is the centre for work related business and enterprise resources for both school and community use.

When Melvyn moved to lead Wymondham College in 2007, Peter Jones took over the Headship of Old Swinford, having already served as Deputy Head. His great love has been Rugby Football, joining the school as Director of Sports and becoming responsible for Rugby development. In his twenty six years at the school, Peter undertook just about every possible role, as a day housemaster, a staff governor, a boarding house tutor, Director of Sport and Deputy Head. Old Swinford has developed a great tradition of Rugby tours, many led by Peter, taking boys to play rugby all over the world. Such tours are usually the preserve of independent schools, backed with parental money. Peter provided boys from a comprehensive state school with the same rich experience.

Back home, Old Swinford Rugby players have excelled in national competitions, reaching the highest level in both the U18 Daily Mail Cup and the National Rugby 7s, playing against the best rugby schools in England, independent and state. During his time as Head, Old Swinford Hospital received capital funding from the Government's scheme to expand successful schools to enable it to grow from 650 to 720 pupils.

I have had the privilege of working with all three of these strong Heads in our struggles in the State Boarding schools to persuade national government to release funs to preserve and develop our boarding places as a national asset. More recently, I have also worked with Melvyn and Peter and their Governors as an External Adviser (EA) and School Improvement Partner (SIP). These last roles grew out of John Major's Conservative Government's commitment to introducing Performance Management for both Heads and Teachers. Eventually it was realised that the whole complex procedure of awarding a pay rise to competent teachers could best be delegated to Heads.

Strong leadership from the Head, effective and 'critically friendly' support from the Governors, very high quality teaching by a committed and professional staff and enough resources to ensure that pupils can enjoy an attractive, safe and supportive environment, all these have ben enjoyed by Old Swinford Hospital for many years. Other Dudley schools look with envy at the school's superb examination results and mutter darkly about '*selecting all our best boys*'. But the great majority of entrants to the school still go as boarders at 11 or 13 from outside Stourbridge. Their parents are attracted to what the school offers and this, no doubt, ensures an entry dominated by families keen for their sons to succeed and affluent enough to pay the £10,950 per year which the school currently charges. The school does not select these boarders on academic ability, apart from a small number who wish to apply for Major or Minor scholarships to cover the boarding fee. Parents select the school.

~

Christ's Hospital and Old Swinford Hospital, two boarding schools, both of which started as charities and both of which still offer outstanding opportunities for boarders today. At Christ's Hospital these were once only available to those children who were nominated by those who paid their fees. Today, parents can apply for a place but there is still a commitment to '*have regard especially to children of families in social, financial or other need*' in the offering of places. The Charitable Foundation behind the school still provides 70% of the total cost and ensures that 82% of pupils are subsidised. At Old Swinford in the state sector, the full costs of teaching and learning are carried by the Government, with parents paying fees solely for boarding. Both schools are still charities, true to their Founders' intentions.

There are two other features shared by both schools. They have an ongoing commitment to *'present to pupils the Christian faith in all its mystery and splendour'* as Christ's Hospital puts it. Old Swinford simply states: *'we are a Christian school, open to children of all faiths and none'*.

Both schools also have strong links with the world of commerce. In Christ's Hospital's case this has always been through the City of London, the commercial heart of England. For Old Swinford, the Founder's wealth was earned from West Midland's commerce and industry, the same business community which continues to support the school's work today. Once, they even shared a 'blue coat' uniform, the full blue coat and yellow stockings which is still supplied by the Independent school today.

6. Royal Connections

Madame Dubois was still puzzled. She had struggled to understand why our state secondary school had boarders. But she did understand our royal connections.

'For your Queen, yes,' she had said. 'That I understand.' She also knew that our school still carried the name of a Tudor boy king, Edward VI.

'Such things are important to you English. We French are proud to have got rid of our kings.'

Whether she would have understood the great variety of schools in England with links with the monarchy is more doubtful. This account of State Boarding schools has already included the three boys' grammar schools which celebrate their royal origins, the Royal Grammar Schools of Lancaster, Colchester and High Wycombe. To add to the confusion, there are many English schools which could equally well call themselves Royal Grammar Schools but choose not to, including the state secondary schools in the two Devon towns of Crediton and Ottery St Mary. The second of these towns has chosen to call its secondary school, King's School, now an Academy, following the example of the nine independent King's Schools scattered across England.

There are also King's Schools in the state sector at Peterborough and Grantham, and there is even a Kings' School, but that is a school for the children of the Armed Forces in Güttersloh, Germany. Apostrophes are very important in English names even if few people these days really understand where to place them!

But there are State Boarding schools which have Royal connections far beyond a name. One was both founded by Royalty and occupies a stately home, set in a park. Gatton

Park lies in a corner of the London green belt between the M25 and the M23. Its six hundred acres were landscaped by Capability Brown in the 1760s and at the centre, the Palladian mansion, Gatton Hall, overlooks a thirty acre lake. Few independent schools can match such opulent surroundings, yet since 1949 this has been the home of a state school, the Royal Alexandra and Albert School (RAAS).

In that year, two orphanages came together to form one school. One started as an Orphan Working School in Hampstead and came under the patronage of Queen Alexandra, the wife of Edward VII. The other, the Royal Albert Orphan Asylum, was set up in memory of Prince Albert, Queen Victoria's husband, after his death. RAAS inherited the links with the Royal family of both these charities and these continue through their current President, HRH the Duke of Gloucester.

The School's Trustees still offer places to pupils both boarding and flexi-boarding who have a boarding need due to their home circumstances. Such pupils become 'Foundationers', provided with financial support towards their boarding fees on a means-tested basis. Currently sixty Foundationers are at the school free of charge. The school also offers 'clergy bursaries' to the children of Church of England clergy covering two thirds of the cost of a boarding place. This reflects the fact that the current Head was himself the son of a clergyman and was supported at an independent boarding school by a generous donor.

The growth and development of RAAS over the last fifteen years is one of the great success stories of State Boarding. Only fifteen years ago the school was an 8-16 school with no Sixth Form and just three hundred and eighty five boarders. Reports from Ofsted had been critical of the low standards of both its discipline and its examination results.

Paul Spencer Ellis, the current Head, was appointed in 2001, having been Vice Principal of Wymondham College. By 2013, RAAS had grown to over eight hundred and twenty pupils from 7 to 18 with four hundred boarders, including flexi-boarders. In 2010, Paul was invited to join a Downing Street reception with Tony Blair for the most improved state schools in the Country.

RAAS is the only state boarding school which has places for Primary age pupils. Forty seven Year 3 children start at seven, with twenty of them coming as full boarders. At Year 7 a further one hundred and thirteen places are offered without academic selection to eleven year olds, including forty six full boarders. At Year 12, Sixth Formers are admitted as both boarders and day students.

For boarders, first priority is given to children who are or have been in the care of a Local Authority. Children of Armed Forces parents in receipt of the CEA are the next priority and children who have a general boarding need are then considered. Siblings of existing pupils and children of staff members are also considered before other applicants for boarding places. By following these policies, RAAS remains true to its charitable origins serving children in boarding need. Paul Spencer Ellis' leadership of the school has been acknowledged by his SBSA colleagues by re-electing him as their Chairman and HMC have elected him to their Conference, one of very few state school Heads to be so included

RAAS is, in Paul's words a *'training ground for real life'*. Many of the pupils have already experienced huge challenges, violence at home, multiple changes of school, poverty and deprivation. Others have lived alongside siblings with ADHT who have made their lives miserable or have parents who simply cannot cope with bringing up a child.

These are the children who need to be at RAAS. Alongside them are an increasing number of young people who are there because their parents like the small classes, the wealth of activities, the tight discipline and the now impressive examination results. These features of the school are hugely attractive to parents in Surrey, where there are no grammar schools and where places in the independent sector are hugely expensive. It costs just £1315 per term to have a son or daughter at RAAS on an extended day place, to live at home overnight but to take advantage of all the facilities and opportunities of a good boarding school. This has been the 'unique selling point' of many SBSA schools and it enables such schools to remain financially viable for the minority of 'needs' boarders for whom the charity was created in the first place.

It costs £3995 a term for a boarding place at RAAS or about £12,000 a year. To keep a child in a Local Authority Residential Care Home costs on average £126,000 a year and a place in a secure unit for a young offender about £400,000 a year. A place at RAAS may provide a training for real life for all. For a sad but significant minority it also saves the Nation huge expense.

~

To the west of RAAS, near Bagshot in Surrey, there is another State Boarding school which has similarly impeccable links with the Royal family. Gordon's School was founded in 1885 by public subscription at the express wish of Queen Victoria as the national memorial to General Gordon, killed at Khartoum. Originally a boys' home for '*necessitous lads*' off the streets of Victorian London, it developed into a boys' and later a co-educational, State Boarding school supported by the Gordon Foundation. The reigning Monarch has been the Patron since Queen Victoria's time.

The school has a full Pipe and Drum Marching Band and a tradition of marching on public parades. This includes an annual Whitehall Parade in London concluding with a service at the Gordon Memorial for which all pupils wear their 'Blues' uniform based on the original version worn at the school in the 1800s.

Gordon's received an outstanding judgement from Ofsted in 2001 and again in 2007, both while Denis Mulkerrin was the Headmaster. He had already been awarded the CBE for services to education. The school has since had similarly glowing reports for boarding in 2013 and for all aspects of the school in 2014. The 2007 report took the very unusual step of starting with a quotation from a parent with two children at the school:

'It is a fantastic school, great staff, great teaching and a lovely happy friendly atmosphere. Bullying is not tolerated and children feel safe as a result. Our children love every second at school and are doing well'.

The report went on to say: *'this encapsulates the opinions of many parents and the inspectors would agree with this view point. Gordon's is an outstanding school in every respect offering a very rich learning experience to its pupils.'*

The school is a non-selective and Voluntary Aided with 670 boys and girls from 11 to 18, including 200 boarders. Under Mulkerrin, the school had a strong emphasis on traditional values, high standards and good discipline. The high quality of teaching in the classroom has been the key to its success because schools are first and foremost centres for learning. In 2008 the percentage of pupils achieving five or more GCSE grades A* to C was 94%. At A-Level, there was a 100% pass rate with two thirds of the grades being either A or B. The school has a very high value added and CVA factor and HM Chief Inspector of Schools lists Gordon's as an 'outstanding school'.

There are four boarding houses and five day houses for pupils who come mainly from the local area. Boarders come from all parts of the United Kingdom with around ten per cent from overseas. With around 550 applications annually for the 100 day places in Year 7, under the Gordon's admissions policy, priority is given first to siblings, followed by day pupils based on radial distance to the main school entrance.

~

RAAS and Gordon's demonstrate that State Boarding schools can be very attractive to relatively affluent parents prepared to pay modest 'day-boarding' fees to enable their children to access the wealth of activities offered by good boarding schools. They are also powerful agents of social mobility for those disadvantaged children for whom they were originally set up.

Every year, these two State Boarding schools with impeccable Royal connections hold a Gordon's vs RAAS rugby match. It may not have the elegance or the social cachet of Eton vs Harrow on the cricket field, but to both these good schools, Gordon's vs RAAS is an important event in the schools' year.

~

There was another school with both Royal connections and boarding places to the north-east of London. In the early 19th Century, a Congregational Minister, Dr Andrew Reed, founded an East London Orphan Asylum and Working School to provide for the children of 'middle class families in distress', those who fell on hard times and faced the hard reality of the workhouse. He gathered together a group of friends to raise the money for a new school building to be sited on Royal land in Wanstead with the agreement of Adelaide, Queen Dowager of William IV. The foundation stone was laid by Prince Albert, consort to Queen Victoria, in 1841.

Sadly, Andrew Reed left the Board of Governors of his new school before the building was completed. They had insisted that the school must teach the Anglican Catechism to the infants. As a non-conformist, he could not accept this and resigned. By 1860, the six hundred capacity of the building had been reached and the school continued until it was renamed again in 1919 by King George V, as the Royal Infant Orphanage. In 1938, it was renamed yet again, becoming the Royal Wanstead School.

After WWII, the school, and its sister girls' school became increasingly dependent on Local Authorities placing children in need in boarding places. By 1965/6, the costs of running the two schools had increased to the point at which Local Authorities were becoming unwilling to buy places and pupil rolls in both schools were falling. In 1971, the Governors had to take the hard decision to close the Royal Wanstead School before the short-fall in fee income caused the collapse of the Charity which owned the school building.

The Royal Wanstead School became the Royal Wanstead Foundation Trust, a charity committed to placing children in boarding need in the most appropriate school, whether that be independent or state. The school premises were sold for a large sum to become the Snaresbrook Crown Court and the money raised was invested to generate an income. This enabled the charity to make grants to support children in need of a boarding place.

Meanwhile, from 1971, another charity had been set up to support pupils at independent schools, mainly Prep Schools, who were in danger of having to leave their schools when their parents' financial circumstances changed. The Joint Educational Trust (JET) was formed by Group Capt. Douglas Bader and Prep School heads and by 2000 was supporting a hundred vulnerable children. By that time, the Royal Wanstead Foundation was supporting two hundred and fifty children.

By 2005, the total number of children being supported by Local Authorities in UK boarding schools had fallen to just fifty. Two year later, the Royal Wanstead Foundation together with the JET helped the Department for Education to launch a new project, the Pathfinder Project, with the aim of increasing the number of children in boarding places supported by Local Authorities. In spite of a lot of effort and good intentions, the project did no significantly increase the numbers of pupils supported in boarding and was wound down from 2009. In 2010, Royal Wanstead and JET merged to form the Royal National Children's Foundation (RNCF).

When the RCNF was set up, the two merging charities were supporting over 340 vulnerable children and young people at some 100 boarding schools and prep day schools throughout the UK. These were mostly children with one or no active parents, who had suffered in their home or family environment and who were below the poverty line. Over the past thirty years, the two charities had helped fund boarding school and independent prep school education for some 2,500 disadvantaged young people. The RCNF research shows that their Assisted Boarding provision transforms the lives and prospects of hundreds of vulnerable young people: they tend to outperform their peers across a range of social, relationship and academic measures because they, quite literally, grasp their golden opportunity with both hands.

Of the children supported by RNCF today, about 25% attend State Boarding schools and 75% are at boarding schools in the independent sector. Currently, a major research study into the efficacy of assisted boarding for children has been commissioned by the RNCF, as a piece of action research carried out by the Buttle Trust, another charity with an interest in supporting children. Children in boarding need will be placed in assisted boarding places, 25% in State and 75% in Independent schools. This is just the sort of research that Royston Lambert had advocated fifty years ago. Those of us who already know the value of such boarding places are confident of the outcome, but it will be good to see the evidence with which to convince those still uncertain.

The Patron of the RNCF is the Princess Royal, who continues the concern for vulnerable children that Dr Andrew Reed so successfully harnessed in the 1840s. Princess Anne writes: *'The two charities share a focused, highly cost-effective approach to providing school-based support for vulnerable young people at risk in their home or family environment. I am pleased to be Patron of The Royal National Children's Foundation and encourage all our supporters and would-be supporters of this combined charity to do everything you can to ensure our continued success in the years ahead.'*

7. The Founding of BSA and SBSA

For boarding schools in England, the publication of Royston Lambert's 1966 research on boarding and the work of the Public Schools Commission did have one major outcome. Faced with the threat of compulsory integration, the boarding schools in the independent sector supported a call from the state sector to meet to consider the future of boarding schools in England.

The call came in June 1966, from Robert Eden, an Essex County Councillor, in the form of an invitation to a meeting at Keble College, Oxford. Eden invited Local Authority officers, the Heads of State schools with boarders, the Heads of Boys Public Schools and of the major Girls Schools to discuss the future of boarding education in the United Kingdom. His meeting was titled: *'Different Approaches to Boarding'* because all who came shared an interest in the challenges of looking after other people's children after the end of the day-school day. Possibly to his surprise, very many of them responded.

Royston Lambert was one of the speakers at that June meeting. His contribution focussed on his claim that there were at least 48,000 children who needed a boarding education. He believed that 30,000 of them were not getting it, even when 'need' was defined in the fairly narrow terms which most Local Education Authorities (LEAs) followed. Lambert said that his report was not an attack on the LEAs although there was an extreme lack of consistency between the practices of different LEAs. The anomalies which he identified derived from the isolation in which LEAs worked and their differing educational priorities.

He argued that there was an urgent need for more co-ordination of policy, procedures and provision by LEAs and that the *present and future scale of the state's involvement should be recognised by a government policy*. What he was advocating was *controlled experiment to see what kinds of boarding would be most suitable for working class people, who derive disproportionally little benefit from the present system*.

At the end of the conference, those taking part agreed that a new Association should be formed bringing together all schools which provided boarding places. It was to represent the interests of all types of boarding schools in England and Wales. The Boarding Schools' Association (BSA) was born and has served boarding schools ever since.

It is the only school association in the UK in which Independent School Heads and State Boarding school Heads meet at annual conferences and serve together on a national committee. That committee elects a Chairman. As a result, the Head of a State Boarding school can find him or herself speaking on behalf of boarding schools in both sectors even though the great majority of boarding schools remain independent. There have been four Chairmen who have served in this way and I was privileged to be one of them.

If the BSA was founded partly because the independent sector perceived the two Newsom Reports to be threats to their continued existence, the anxiety proved to be unfounded. The BSA Chairman in the year the second report was published predicted that 1968 Newsom Report was a 'dead duck'. He was right. The Independent schools continued much as before. But BSA established a key role in encouraging high standards of boarding welfare and providing good professional development of boarding staff through sharing good boarding practice. BSA also set out to provide information for parents and others about boarding and boarding schools, to publish research on boarding and to maintain a dialogue with national and local government on issues which impact on boarding schools.

Following the Keble Conference, over 190 organisations joined BSA, 134 independent schools, 28 maintained and other schools, 22 local education authorities and a collection of other bodies including the Department of Education and Science, the Methodist Education Committee, the Oxford University Education Department and the Independent Association of Prep Schools. For the first time, boarding education in England and Wales had an organisation to promote and defend all boarding schools, boys', girls', and mixed, primary and secondary, state maintained and independent, selective and non-selective.

The Keble College Conference participants asserted that their aim would be to *'let it be known that many children from all types of homes actually need boarding and that others would benefit in varying degrees from some boarding experience'*. They agreed to make *'correcting the idea that boarding education has any social class connotation'*, their first priority.

Fifty years later, it is hard to see that this has been successful as most people in England still equate boarding with Independent schools serving affluent families!

The second aim of that first meeting was *'Fostering co-operation and co-ordination between all kinds of school on a local basis ... with the object of exploring the possibility of amalgamated classes, teacher exchanges and fuller use of existing facilities all round by common participation'*.

Again, Lambert had found a lack of any meaningful degree of co-operation or co-ordination between schools on a local level and an astonishing lack of any sort of national data-base of information about boarding in the Maintained sector. The Government did publish a 'List of Independent Schools (List 70)' and a 'List of Direct Grant Grammar Schools (List 73)' which parents and others could easily access and but there was no equivalent list for state schools maintained by the LEAs.

By 1974, there was still no national policy on boarding education from either main political party and it was still assumed by most people in the UK that 'boarding' meant the Independent sector. BSA appointed Dr Ewan Anderson, a former Housemaster and an academic at Durham University to conduct research on boarding and invited him in 1978 to run a National Clearing House for boarding places in the State sector. A concern in boarding schools for good in-service training for staff involved in boarding houses led to the publication by BSA of the first guidance booklet; *'The Housemaster and the Law'*, which went through seventeen editions.

Attempts by BSA to persuade national government to develop a policy on boarding continued to fail in spite of publications like the polemical leaflet *'Boarding for Britain'*, although government funding for the Clearing House was secured. There are some of us who have served as State Boarding Heads who would now argue that lack of an overall Government policy on the role of State boarding has actually worked to our advantage, allowing enterprising Heads and Governors to develop State Boarding schools on a wide variety of models.

The issue of unmet boarding need against a decline in boarding provision led the BSA to undertake a research project and report in 1987 *'Children in Boarding Need'*, which attempted to quantify such 'need'. The Report suggested that

70% of boarders in maintained schools were there because of a 'need' and nearly half those in the Independent sector were in similar 'need'. Between 1964 and 1987, the State Boarding sector had shrunk from about 12,000 boarding places to just over 7,000 places with no discernible shrinkage in 'need'. It has since shrunk to about 3,800 and then risen to about 5,000 places. Clearly other factors such as Local Authority attitudes, lower parental support for boarding and funding issues were involved.

In 1989, for the first time, the Children Act placed a statutory responsibility on all Independent boarding schools to ensure that they met minimum standards and provided specific safe-guards for children in their care. The implementation of the Act was reinforced by regular inspections by Local Authority Social Service teams – the first such regular professional contact between the two worlds of Social Service Inspectors and Independent boarding schools.

In spite of the fears of many schools and the lack of experience of many teams, the principles which the Act endorsed came to be accepted and even welcomed in most boarding schools. Tony Little, the former Head of Eton, told the 2014 Conference of State Boarding Schools that the introduction of the Children Act 1989 was, in his view, one of the best things to happen to boarding schools. Not everybody would have agreed with him when the Act was first implemented!

By the start of the 1990s, the National Clearing House for boarding places was seen by many Heads of State schools with boarders to have outlived its usefulness. More and more decisions were being transferred from the Local Authorities to the schools. Many of the State Boarding schools had taken Grant Maintained status to break away from Local Authority control. They were frustrated with their lack of direct involvement in the recruitment of boarders at national level which the Clearing House implied.

The Heads of State Boarding schools met in London to discuss the future of Maintained School boarding in their schools. It was May Day 1990 and many of us wondered if boarding in our schools would survive for much longer. Some, like Caistor Grammar School faced strong pressure from Governors and staff to close boarding and use the premises to increase day numbers as there were very many parents keen to get their children into a grammar school but not keen to send them as boarders. Others of us were finding it more and more difficult to justify spending time and effort on what was very much a minority activity in our schools. All of us were frustrated that there was no national marketing strategy for our boarding places – we were still the 'best kept secret' of the maintained school system.

Before we all set off that evening to return to our schools, we agreed to try to set up just such a strategy. John Pugsley of Beaminster School offered to make a start by setting up a 'Parents' Guide to Maintained School Boarding' to which we would all contribute a section for our own school. On the Hull train from King's Cross, those of us from Grantham, Louth, Caistor, and Bridlington, tried to work out what a marketing association might look like, based on the model of the Independent Schools Information Service (ISIS). After several cans of Newcastle Brown Ale, our strategy was set out on the back of an A4 envelope and by the time many of us had left the train at Newark, STABIS, the State Boarding Information Service, had been invented. When the BSA met in annual conference at Low

Wood a week later, the Executive Committee agreed to endorse the formation of STABIS and to close the Local Authority Clearing House system.

From this modest beginning, STABIS soon gained some credibility, with the publication of the 'Parent's Guide to State School Boarding'. We decided that no-one knew what the 'maintained sector' was but they knew what 'state schools' were! The BSA published the first 'Parents' Guide to State School Boarding' and then negotiated financial support from the Department of Education to continue the publication and distribution of this guide. STABIS members continued to be members of BSA. But the Heads involved eventually became convinced that the name STABIS still did not make its purpose sufficiently clear. They agreed in the late 1990s to rename their association the State Boarding Schools' Association (SBSA). All SBSA schools remained in membership of BSA. Sadly, by that time, State School Boarding in Grantham, Caistor, Louth, and Bridlington, the boarding houses in the schools which were the inventors of STABIS on that Hull train, had closed.

By 1991, frustration with falling boarding rolls had reached the point of BSA and National ISIS agreeing a national boarding promotion campaign, starting with a National Boarding Conference in London. Baroness Warnock gave the keynote speech. The event was well supported by the schools' Heads and Governors and attracted some national publicity. It also marked the start of a 'National Boarding Week' including promotional events in boarding schools in both sectors all over the country. The Week set out to promote boarding, create local publicity, boost morale and re-brand what schools were offering as 'modern boarding'. This had an emphasis on 'a home away from home', good food, colourful duvets and caring staff. It was a long way from what Sarkozy has since described as '*austere boarding*'. But sadly, boarding numbers in both the UK Independent and State sectors went on falling through the 1990s.

BSA's commitment to effective in-service training for all staff involved in boarding was further strengthened in 1993 with the appointment of a National Training Co-ordinator and a link with Roehampton University. These developments led to a programme of professional training and development for all boarding staff in schools across all sectors. This focus on a professional approach to working in boarding schools remains a key part of the Association's activity today and has radically improved the day to day experience of many boarders. BSA also continues to run an annual programme of national conferences for Heads, Deputies, House Staff and Matrons and School Nurses, to share best practice and current research in boarding schools.

It was not surprising that it was a leader of Essex County Council who had convened the Keble meeting and hence the first BSA conference. His Local Authority was a major contributor to the provision of State boarding, with ten schools at that time providing a total of 916 boarding places. Six were grammar schools, three secondary moderns and, unusually, Essex maintained two primary schools with boarding places.

Fifty years later, what has happened to this rich provision of LEA maintained boarding in Essex? Of the ten schools from 1964, just one state school in the County still has boarders, the Royal Grammar School in Colchester, a highly selective boys' school with just thirty boarding places restricted to 6th form students. Over the last fifty years, one

County has gone from providing 916 boarding places in its schools to zero for 5-16 children. Just thirty 16+ places have survived at Colchester RGS. If Royston Lambert was right in claiming that there were 48,000 children in the UK in 1964 needing a boarding place, and if Essex was providing 916 places towards meeting that need, how is it that today there is no state boarding for 5-16 pupils in Essex?

To be fair, there is state boarding which has Essex roots in neighbouring Hertfordshire, as the Hockerill Anglo-European College near Bishop's Stortford grew out of a combination of the Essex secondary modern boarding schools. But the question remains. Has the need, if it ever really existed, simply gone away or have parents simply turned their backs on boarding and chosen other opportunities for their children?

The national decline is less dramatic than Essex's but it is still massive. Across England in 1964, there were 128 schools with boarding provision maintained by LEAs and the number was actually growing. By 1991, there were still 61 state maintained schools with boarding places according to a report to Parliament, although 16 of these had fewer than 20 boarders. By 1994, the number of schools had fallen to 42, and by the early 2000s had reached a low point of 32 schools. Thanks to the efforts of Heads and Governors, State Boarding survived in these 32 schools and by 2010, the number of state schools with boarders started to increase. It is now heading towards 40. Whereas it was the LEAs who controlled state boarding in the past, the system is now firmly in the hands of Heads and Governors.

The 1966 Keble College meeting which led to the founding of the BSA attracted many Heads from the independent sector. If the state sector schools at that time lacked any sort of national co-ordination and information system, the independent schools faced other threats. Dick Davison of ISIS has pointed out that the BSA was *'founded at a time when the most lethal threats to boarding schools were more political than economic'*. That would explain why so many leading independent schools responded to the invitation of a Local Authority Councillor to discuss the future of boarding and why so many agreed to join the new Association. They have been fully involved alongside their State Boarding colleagues ever since and include the Prep Schools in the IAPS, the Girls' Schools in GSA, the smaller and less well known schools which are in ISAI and SHMIS, and the Headmasters' and Headmistresses' Conference, HMC.

8. Going comprehensive

The typical origin of State Boarding –
an Eighteenth century Headmaster's house in which
boys boarded in the attics, and a Victorian wing of
dormitories, in this case at Louth

Between and 1960s and the 1980s, England's state secondary schools went through a process of huge upheaval, from the 1944 Act system of grammar schools and secondary moderns, into comprehensive schools. It was a change which many teachers, especially those who had been privileged to teach able pupils in the O and A level classes of grammar schools, found very traumatic. The merits or otherwise of this reorganisation process are still being debated today.

~

After leaving the King's School, Worcester in 1968, I first spent four years as an Education Officer in the service of the Government of Uganda, teaching science in a mixed state boarding school in the far north-west of the country near the borders with the Congo and the Sudan. Contractually, I was the 'loyal servant', first of Milton Obote and then of Idi Amin, but in reality I served the young men and women who boarded at the secondary school in Arua, and then their contemporaries who were at the school

94

attached to Makerere University in Kampala. As a teaching experience, it was always interesting, usually rewarding, occasionally frustrating and once or twice, terrifying.

~

I returned to a teaching post in Northumberland and I went through the process of secondary reorganisation from the last year of a boys' grammar school to a very successful mixed 13-18 High School with a very large Sixth Form, led by a strong Head backed by an efficient Local Authority. They had planned the change together over a number of years and had used the capital funding which went with re-organisation to provide new buildings for the new start. King Edward VI School, Morpeth, admitted boys and girls from a wide swathe of mid-Northumberland between the Scottish border and the coastal coal field, and served them very effectively. It continues to do so today.

~

Coming back from Uganda in 1972, I could have simply forgotten about our time in a boarding school on the Equator and got on with the pressing need to adapt to the challenge of teaching the young people of the North East. But I found that our experience under Obote and Amin was in many ways still very relevant to working in England again. We had learnt a great deal of value about boarding schools from our time in two Ugandan schools whose pupils really were 'State School boarders' even if of a more exotic variety than those we would meet over the next thirty years.

The tide of comprehensive re-organisation which had moved north through Northumberland in the 1970s was planned to reach Morpeth in September 1973, a year after our arrival. This meant that I only had one month of teaching as Head of Chemistry at the 11-18 King Edward VI Grammar School for Boys in Morpeth before all the staff were invited to apply for posts in the new 13-18 King Edward VI High School. It was to be formed from the two single sex grammar schools and the two town secondary modern schools in Morpeth. The latter two schools were to be combined at the same time to form an 8-13 Middle School for the town. A small rural middle school, the Dr Thomlinson Middle School, in Rothbury about fifteen miles to the North West served the Coquet Valley running up almost to the Scottish border.

The Head of the new High School had already been appointed. George Chapman had been Head of Ashington Grammar School before becoming the last Head of the Morpeth Boys' Grammar. It was George who had summoned me for interview off the flight from Uganda and offered me the post in his school, my first foothold back into UK education. 'Just play your cards right,' was his advice when I was called for interview for the posts in the new school. I must have done, as the Governors offered me the combined school Head of Chemistry post, much to the fury of the Girls' School Head of Department who had been in post for years and clearly thought that this wild colonial upstart would surely not be considered ahead of him. We had a year to re-establish a working relationship before the new school started the following September, by which time we knew we could work together.

Northumberland had planned the change to 13-18 comprehensive High Schools very carefully with a series of geographical areas from the south to the north changing in turn to ensure that the later areas learnt from the experience of change in the earlier. The County had successfully bid for capital building funds for the whole programme right at the start and Morpeth was about half-way through the programme. As a result, both Girls' and Boys' Grammar Schools in Morpeth moved into new buildings on the King Edward VI School site two years before the change. When the change to create the new school came, the only additional development was to unlock the doors of the Science department prep rooms which formed the central link between two buildings.

Many of the Secondary Modern staff had decided to move with their 13-15 pupils to join the High School and they were welcomed and fully integrated into the combined staff team. We thought of ourselves as one staff from day one and as the School Leaving Age was raised in the same year as we were re-organised, the expertise of the teachers who knew our new 15 year olds now staying with us until after their 16th birthday was invaluable.

Although I had never taught boys and girls who were not of Grammar School ability, I was keen to lead from the front and found myself devising science courses for all abilities. I soon learnt that the Morpeth ROSLA groups were much more interested in me as a young male teacher with a Southern accent than the finer points of Chemistry, especially as I had a young and very pregnant wife and a French car with red temporary number plates. One of the boys christened me 'Jacques Cousteau' because he'd seen the underwater explorer's films 'on the Tele'.

The girls quite enjoyed the modules on 'Chemistry for Hairdressing' and 'The Science of Make-up' while the boys had a great time trying to mix ingredients for hair-oil that might just pass for their favourite product: *A little dab of*

Brylcreem on your hair gives you the Brylcreem jump in the air' 'as they sing on the Tele, Sir!' Meanwhile, I also continued to enjoy teaching A level Chemistry to the more academic older pupils.

~

One spring Friday afternoon I got carried away by this enthusiasm for all ability science and allowed some boys and girls in my set to finish off their practical work after the school bell had gone. A very stern Deputy Head appeared at the lab door. I was in real trouble having failed to understand the significance of 'the Friday Rothbury bus'. Sitting on lab stools were two grinning teenagers, Alan and Maggie Robson. They knew all about the Friday Rothbury bus.

'But your work was so interesting, Sir, we just forgot!' Maggie assured me with a smirk.

'Just forgot, Sir, honest,' her twin brother chorused. 'I suppose you'll have to take us home, since we've missed the bus from being in your lesson.'

I checked with the Deputy Head at the door, keen to get off home for the weekend.

'Well, I suppose you could do that – we'll have to 'phone your parents and tell them that you'll be late.'

'That'll be fine, Miss. They'll not be worried.'

So I and the Robson twins got into the Jacques Cousteau machine, the Renault 4 with the French number plates, and set out for Rothbury.

'You do know where we live?' asked Maggie. 'It's not in Rothbury. On a Friday, see, the Rothbury bus from school runs all the way up the Dale to Barrowburn where we live. It takes ages – that's why they let us board in Thomlinson's.'

It was fifteen miles up the Wooler road and across on the B road to Rothbury. From there the road up Coquetdale ran past Harbottle and deep into the Northumberland National Park. On the left hand bank of the little river, dire red warning notices told us not to stray into the MOD Live Firing Range which covered the hills across to Otterburn Camp. The scattered sheep and the calling curlews did not seem too bothered about the risks. 'What's it like when they're using the ranges?' I asked the twins, by now nodding off in the back of the car.

'Doesn't bother us much, but we lost a wether last year. Silly bogger was trying to tup a yow and fell off ont'a live shell and 'poof', that was it – took the yow with 'im!'

We eventually got to Barrowburn and the stone farmhouse where they lived. Their mother was waiting for us framed in the doorway, arms folded.

'Yer dozy pair,' she said. 'Fancy not telling 'im you'd miss the bus. You'll stop for a bite of tea, Mr 'aden. It's all set.'

Later that evening, as I drove back down the dale and through the peaceful little town of Rothbury on my way home to Morpeth, I thought how tough those families living at the top of Coquetdale had to be. They farmed large flocks of sheep across the flanks of the Cheviot Hills with uncertain prices for both their lambs and their wool. From the age of five, their children had to go down the Dale in all weathers, past Alwinton to the hamlet of Harbottle where the tiny First School is still there, hanging on with about twenty children. When the County set up a three level school system for their area, they opted to have their children board at Rothbury, still within Coquetdale, rather than have them live in Morpeth in the valley of the Wansbeck. That was foreign territory to the Coquetdale folk.

It meant that all the 13-18 students had to travel by bus the fifteen miles each way into the town, but that was their preference. Today, boarding at Dr Tomlinson's CE Middle School has stopped so High School pupils from Coquetdale must have other arrangements for schooling.

We had five very happy years at Morpeth working in what was and is today a very good school, a comprehensive with a very large 6th Form, a strong local community behind it and strong leadership. After three years, Northumberland Local Authority generously allowed me to take a term off from my post to start a B Phil degree at the University of York which I enjoyed enormously. Jenny meanwhile was able to cover most of my classes at King Edward VI School while looking after our two young sons. I completed the B Phil course and was awarded the degree and started to look around for a promoted post.

The most competitive promotion step in teaching is often from Head of Department to Deputy Head and I applied for about thirty posts before I started to get interviews. All the posts were in mixed comprehensive schools as I knew that this was the type of school I wanted to serve in. They were all also in market towns as we had both developed a real affection for communities of about 8,000 to 15,000 people, large enough to support good schools and small enough to be places where you could get to know a good number of local people. I tried to find a state school with boarders but there were none which advertised posts.

~

Then one day in 1981, I was appointed to a Deputy Head post in North Yorkshire. When the contract arrived, I found that I was to become the 'Senior Mistress of Northallerton Grammar School', an odd offer as I was clearly not female and the school was not a grammar school.

Northallerton had been reorganised on comprehensive grounds two years earlier. The ancient Grammar School of the town, founded 1303, had become a fourteen form entry Upper School from 14 to 18. North Yorkshire in their wisdom had appointed an experienced Head to develop Northallerton Grammar as a comprehensive school. Unfortunately, he had no experience of comprehensive schools, having been the Head of a very small grammar school. He set up a novel solution to how best to run a fourteen form entry comprehensive school. All the experienced teachers, including all the Heads of Department were given all the Sixth Form A level teaching and all the O level sets in years 10 and 11 – they effectively continued to teach in a grammar school. Because these pupils took eight subjects to O level, they were referred to as the Eight Subject Band.

All the pupils from the secondary modern school, and there were twice as many of them as the ex-grammar pupils, were designated the Six Subject Band. To teach them, the Head recruited a team of young inexperienced teachers to join the band of embittered staff who had failed to become Heads of Department in the new 11-14 school. It was a recipe for educational disaster but most of the staff tried to make the new system work. My post as 'Senior Mistress' had a second line – and Head of Upper School. I asked the Head just what this designation meant.

'Well,' he said with a smile. 'With such a large year group, we thought that we should have two levels of leadership. Each year has a Head of Year to work with a team of tutors for pastoral care, one for year 10, one for year 11 and one for the 6th Form. I've asked Peter, the other male deputy, to be Head of Lower School, which will cover Year 10, and I've appointed you to be Head of Upper School, which will cover Year 11 – oh, and the 6th Form,' he added as an afterthought.

'That seems a lot of young people,' I pondered. 'Four hundred and twenty in year 11 and another three hundred and fifty in the 6th Form, does that mean that I'm responsible for all seven hundred and seventy of them – that's more than two thirds of the school!'

'That's right,' he said. 'But don't worry about the 6th Form, they're not much of a discipline problem.'

And that's how his 'senior mistress' became 'master in charge of discipline' for all of years 11, 12 and 13. If anyone in Year 10 misbehaved, and very many did, their teachers would send them to Peter, to be punished. He, being a former boxing blue, was a sufficiently intimidating presence to have little repeat business. He favoured a gym shoe as his weapon of choice. As a much less impressive executioner, I was told by the Head that the staff would expect me to use a cane to have any influence over Y11 behaviour. Our offices were at opposite ends of the long corridor which ran through the old part of the school. Soon my lengthening break-time punishment queue threatened to meet his, nearer and nearer to his end of the corridor.

~

Boys' schools had always resorted to caning to impose discipline and I well remember my own experience as a pupil on the occasion that I received six of the best, aged twelve, in the last year of Prep school. We had a particularly incompetent English teacher who was fond of leaning out of the sash window in his classroom which overlooked the path down to the games field. One hot afternoon he was leaning out as usual and enjoying the view, enhanced by the cleavage of the French Assistante walking past below. I and the boy the other side of the window unhooked the rope holding up the heavy sash and gently lowered it across his back. By the time it touched him, it was too late. Our English teacher was pinned to the window sill. Eventually, of course, we released him, livid with rage and bent on revenge as he sent us to the Headmaster to be caned. We both felt that the price had been worth it.

~

So when it became my turn to be the school wielder of the cane, I knew, roughly, what to do and, roughly, what the tariff should be. Most weeks it would be the same cheerful rogues from Year 11 who were sent to me, often by the same members of staff, to receive the same short lecture on growing up and the same punishment. Interestingly they never seemed to bear me a grudge, even though it was me wielding the cane. On Saturdays, the same boys would be serving on Northallerton market fruit and veg stalls and always greeted me with a cheery 'Morning, Sir, cabbages is good today,' or whatever they recommended. Often the most hardened rogues would slip an extra spud into my bag with a conspiratorial grin. 'No hard feelings, eh, Sir!'

~

By 1980, three things finally convinced me that I would have to stop hitting boys with a cane. Firstly, I was sure that I was having little effect on the behaviour of my regular customers, the group of boys queuing each week in the corridor, by ritually hitting them. They actually preferred to be caned as a punishment rather than having to serve long detentions. I was becoming increasingly unwilling to oblige them.

Then there was the need to find a witness for each caning, who had to sign the punishment book. It always seemed to me that the staffroom would magically empty as soon as I appeared towards the end of break. Too often, the only person left was a young lady student teacher or young lady colleague who had to be asked to sit in my office and witness the punishment so that she could sign the book. I kept a bottle of ready-mixed gin and tonic in my desk drawer to offer those whose nerves needed to be stiffened before returning to their classroom. This could not go on. I talked to Peter and discovered that he was even more keen than I was to end the practice. So we saw the Head and told him that neither of his Deputies was prepared to continue punishing boys with cane or slipper from the 1st September 1980 – or whatever date we chose.

The Governors, a little reluctantly, agreed the change as none of them was willing to beat children. The new policy was announced to the staff at the summer staff meeting, just before the Y11 students went on examination leave – perfect timing! Corporal punishment ended in our school. Six years later it was banned in all state schools, but only by a majority in Parliament of just one vote, 231 to 230. In the independent sector, caning and slippering went on until an amendment to the 1998 Schools Standards and Framework Bill banned all corporal punishment in schools in England, although the Scots and the Northern Irish took their time to ban the practice. At Northallerton Grammar School, when we returned in September 1980, school discipline did not collapse. Peter and I found other ways of supporting our colleagues as they struggled with disruptive pupils.

~

By 1982, having been an Acting Head once, very briefly in Uganda, and a Deputy Head for nearly five years, I felt that I was ready to try to convince Governors and Local Authorities that I could be trusted with one of their schools. To add credibility to my feeling, I completed an excellent Open University Management in Education course, a precursor to the NPQH, and looked for opportunities. Jenny was not keen to move again, but was prepared to let me at least try. I was invited for interviews in Louth in Lincolnshire and on the next day, to Bradford in Yorkshire.

'You'd better get the Louth job because I'm not going to Bradford.'

There had been riots that summer in Bradford. From our experience in Uganda, we had both had quite enough of rioting young people to last a lifetime.

~

The Louth Governors asked me whether I 'suffered fools gladly', having read a reference about my Northallerton role;

perhaps they were looking for a successor to their 1552 Head, John Goodall, portrayed birching boys in the school's badge.

Taking over the Headship of King Edward VI School, Louth, was very simple. Shortly before my first term started I met the retiring Head, Donald Witney, in his office in the Lodge to be briefed about the school. We had been in touch since the interviews and I knew that he was held in great affection in the town. He had led the school for over twenty years, from the boys' grammar school to which he was appointed through all the amalgamations and reorganisations of the 1960s and 1970s. There was even a new affectionate gargoyle on the Parish Church in his image. Donald had been at that first boarding meeting at Keble College and had served as the Chairman of BSA from 1970 to 1972.

~

King Edward VI School, Louth, was the 14-18 part of the 'Louth Plan', a unique secondary system invented by four Heads to preserve their schools and yet be 'comprehensive'. Three secondary modern schools became 'High Schools' with Y7 entry without the 11+ assessment. At 14, about 25% of the full year group from each High School transferred to Y10 in King Edward VI by a system of 'guided parental choice' and then stayed there through a large 6th Form. The Plan avoided closing any school, needed minimum capital expenditure and was operated collectively by the four Heads under a joint Governing Body.

Donald had explained all this to me on a previous visit and the only thing left to do was the actual handover. He fished out a large cardboard box from under his desk. On the side was written S.O.B.

'I've found it convenient,' he explained, 'to file all the non-urgent communications from County Offices and the DofE in this for the last few months. You'll find it's all here. I call it my '*Some Other Bugger*' file. Good luck, old man.' And with that he handed me the keys to his office and went off to join his wife for lunch at the pub.

~

I had two mishaps in my first week as Head in Louth. At the first staff meeting of the term when, in an attempt to create a relaxed atmosphere I occupied a comfortable chair and balanced a mug of very hot coffee on one arm. Promptly forgetting that it was there, I managed to tip the contents into my lap. The meeting minutes duly recorded that '*the Head left the meeting temporarily to change his trousers*'.

When I first moved to Louth, Jenny and our sons stayed in Northallerton while I lived temporarily in a rented room. It was in the empty girls' boarding house of one of the High schools and had been the Assistant Matron's bedroom. That room nearly witnessed the end of my career in Louth.

One very frosty night in my first month at the school, the hospitable Head of the other High School invited me out for a 'bite of supper and a glass or two'. Several glasses of his excellent malt whisky later, I made my way back to my temporary home in the Assistant Matron's bedroom in the empty girls' boarding house. I reached the boarding house front door and realised that the key was not in my pocket. It was a very cold night.

Looking up at the Assistant Matron's bedroom window I wondered how easy it would be to climb up a drain pipe and see if the bedroom window could be opened from the outside. I decided to try. Half way up the drain pipe, I had a mental picture of the headline in the local paper next week: *'New Head found dead of hypothermia with broken leg under Assistant Matron's bedroom window, full story on page 3.'*

Thankful for this warning, I slid back down the pipe and decided to shoulder charge the front door. Fortunately, it burst open and my reputation was, for the moment, preserved except for an explanation to the High School caretaker as to why he needed to fit a new lock.

~

After these interesting mishaps in my first weeks in the school, I needed to understand the needs of our boarders. King Edward VI School was typical of state day schools in rural areas which still had provision for boarders. Originally, the boys had lived in the Head's house with its Victorian dormitory wing. In the 1970s, they were moved into a large Georgian mansion which had been used as a Home for the Blind – it still had the hand-rails which had helped the residents to find their way around the House and Garden. The House was run by a wonderful couple who brought up their own two children surrounded by about thirty boys, appearing always to be both relaxed and understanding. This House had all the warmth and friendliness that my own boarding experience had lacked.

The boys loved being there. What had been the main bedrooms of the grand family who had first owned it became dormitories for up to five boys. The attics where the maids had lived became the study bedrooms for 6th Formers. There were no House prefects and no one was every caned or slippered. The senior boys were expected to help the juniors with everything from impromptu games of football in the garden to solving the mysteries of maths homework.

This house was popular with the boys but hopelessly uneconomic. The Blind Society owners before the school took it over seemed not to have noticed the crumbling walls and chimneys of their Listed Building – clearly their residents were equally unaware. Unfortunately, parents visiting their sons were more observant and more critical. Trying to maintain the two hundred year old fabric, to decorate the interior and to ensure that all the essential modern alarm systems worked became increasingly impossible out of the fees which we charged.

Eventually, the Governors were forced into a decision to close the House but boarding for boys at the school was saved. At about the same time, the local Health Board had decided to close their maternity hospital which was immediately adjacent to the main school site. This building consisted of a solidly built Victorian hospital linked by an umbilical corridor to the 20th century maternity unit and nurses' quarters behind.

After much discussion with the Charity Commissioners, it was agreed that the Foundation Governors could sell the boys' boarding house provided that the same capital sum was reinvested in the old hospital, a property of roughly equivalent value. This preserved the historic capital endowment of the charity and enabled the school to move the boys from a disused blind home to a disused maternity hospital. The key feature of both was that they included about thirty beds.

The girls' boarding house was even more complicated both in staffing and in premises. The twenty five girls were housed in two beautiful Georgian mansions in what Pevsner called the best street in Louth. The premises were once used to house the Girls' Grammar School and were owned by the same Foundation as the boys' school. Living in this elegant splendour were the Housemistress, her teenage son and twenty five girl boarders. Her flat was part of the large house occupied by the younger girls. Across on the other side of the central hall, her teenage son's bed-sitting room was adjacent to the senior girls – *'just to keep an eye on them,'* as the Housemistress explained to me when my eyebrows expressed amazement on first discovering this novel arrangement.

Apparently my predecessor had offered her the job of running the girls' boarding house when her son had been away at a mixed independent boarding school in the South. It was accepted that he could join her when he too needed a home in the school holidays. All of this was entirely reasonable. When the arrangement had been going on for some years, he was apparently asked to leave his boarding school for reasons which were never very clear to me, and so needed a home in term-time too. He was using his room in the girls' boarding house right through the year, term-time and holidays.

This arrangement seemed to me to break every principle of good boarding pastoral care but to my surprise, had never been challenged. He was eighteen when I took over the school and clearly enjoyed living well away from his mother, next to the 6th Form girls. Fortunately they found him very unattractive and the feeling was mutual. Whatever he might have thought of their charms, he was much more interested in stripping his motorcycle engine and spreading the parts all over his bedroom floor.

It took me over a year to untangle this arrangement. The Housemistress did not find my leadership of the school very comfortable. She agreed a generous early retirement package which the Governors thought far too expensive. I thought it very good value and much cheaper than the cost of being sued by parents or being taken to an industrial tribunal for unfair dismissal.

In her place came a couple who created as warm an atmosphere in the House as the boys enjoyed in theirs and still found time to bring up their five young children. Both couples welcomed into their Houses teams of non-resident Tutors to cover supervision duties and both wives served as matrons. For the rest of my time at the school I could relax, knowing that both boys and girls were in very good hands. Recruiting enough boarders remained a challenge but once they were with us, they had a very good experience of boarding. Many were at that time supported by County Council means tested grants.

King Edward VI School at that time was in many ways a unique and successful school. In Y10 and Y11, we had just four classes of relatively able and keen young people, boys and girls. They provided our team of very able teachers with good opportunities to do what they loved most – teach their subject. With a 6th Form of nearly three hundred, more than half the total school role, we had a student body heavily skewed to the more adult end of the school range. Pimply teenagers of 14 to 16 aspired to be 'grown up' and, given the greater maturity of the girls, most of them were. It was the sort of school through which the sons and daughters of the teaching staff could happily move without any pressure from an anti-success element. Our two sons both flourished there.

~

There was also a lot to do. Donald's benevolent reign had established a culture of scholarship and a very warm community but what was effective and accepted in the 1960s

111

and 1970s was being challenged by the 1980s. Prefects, school blazers, speech days, the CCF and corporal punishment, had all gone and in their place had come a liberal and relaxed approach to pupil leadership, celebrating success and ensuring good discipline. Most of this worked well but there were those on the Governors and the staff who looked back to an earlier more rigorous regime and lobbied for change. I had no great love of Prefects, school blazers or Speech Days and I had no colleagues willing to staff a CCF, but I was interested in discipline, especially of the 'self' variety.

Our examination results, always strong, crept upwards as the Heads of Department began to share their best practice. The convention that each teacher's classroom was an island untroubled by visits from the Head and Deputies broke down. We knew that we would never get the results that Caistor Grammar School, just up the road, achieved as we were nothing like as selective as they were. Their 11+ entry drew applicants from all over the Grimsby/South Humberside conurbation and they could set a pass mark that ensured that only the most able got in whether they lived in Caistor or not. Our Y10 entry was limited to those pupils from the High School Y9s whose parents applied to transfer to us at 14, plus a small number of boarding places. In that sense we remained true to the school's 1551 Charter, when the young King's advisers decreed that the Free Grammar School of King Edward VI should endure for ever for the education of boys and youth of the town.

So we resisted the pressure to admit boys and girls from a wide area, which would have pushed some Louth pupils out and admitted those pupils from the local community who wanted to join us. While all the Heads were happy to work together in the interests of the system as a whole, it worked well.

As new Heads joined us and as school funding focused more sharply on '*age-weighted pupil units*' the tensions between us increased. The High School staff had always, quite reasonably, resented losing their most able pupils at 14 to King Edward VI School and not being able to start their own 6th Forms. For ten more years, the system held together with increasing difficulty until national legislation designed to stop City Authorities appointing one Governing Body to run all their secondary schools outlawed our Louth Plan Joint Governors. With separate governors and ambitious Heads it was inevitable that the Plan would break down.

Four separate secondary schools came into existence, two of which then developed their own 6th Forms. The next stage, the re-introduction of the 11+ test for selective entry and the re-organisation of King Edward VI School back into its historic role as an 11-18 Grammar School, was approved in the dying days of John Major's government before Tony Blair's Labour victory in 1997. The school may therefore have the distinction of being reorganised from a grammar school to be part of a comprehensive system only to be reorganised again after over thirty years back into a grammar school.

~

It was while we were in Louth that I followed Donald Whitney's interest in the Boarding Schools' Association. Having chaired STABIS and been on the national committee for BSA, I was elected Chairman of BSA for 1990 to 1992 and became heavily involved in the promotion of boarding across both sectors in National Boarding Week. It was a huge privilege to work alongside distinguished independent school Heads like David McMurray of Oundle and Audrey Butler of Queenswood. David had led his school from a very successful boys' boarding school to become an equally successful boarding school for both boys and girls while Audrey had remained utterly convinced, and convincing, of the benefits of all girls' schools. State school Heads very rarely get the opportunity to work with the leaders of HMC and GSA, the Girls' Schools Association, but this was possible through BSA's mission of promoting boarding opportunities across all UK schools, independent and state.

~

While I was still Chairman of BSA and happily enjoying my tenth year at King Edward VI School, Louth, I had a 'phone call from Ron Wolsey, the Principal of Wymondham College in Norfolk. His Governors, he said, would be pleased if I could come down to Wymondham with my wife to have a look at his College.

Driving into the Wymondham College campus today, it is difficult to believe what it was like in 1992. The roads are still the same as are the six main school boarding blocks – 'Colditz blocks' the boarders used to call them. New, Cavell, Fry, Peel, Lincoln and Kett, each a hollow square of three floors of day rooms and dormitories, they were functional and solid. They were and still are the heart of the College. There were other permanent buildings, a huge brick Sports Hall and an industrial shed of a dining hall. Near to the road to Morley village, the caretaker's house guarded the second access road. Next door, the Principal's house sat in isolation like the Commanding Officer's quarters of an RAF station.

On the far side of the site towards the acres of playing fields, a music and drama building lay next to a housing estate of semis for the staff. The College had a very fine library, a memorial to the founder Sir Lincoln Ralphs, and an excellent set of science labs. It also had a huge brick water tower and a sewage farm, which functioned well if the weather was not too dry and the wind stayed in the west! Otherwise, the buildings were all WWII temporaries, Nissen huts, HORSA huts and even some wartime pre-fabs.

It was the huts which were the famous feature of Wymondham College. Spread across the foreground beside the road, and lined up in other parts of the site, twenty full sized Nissen huts were gently rusting away. For nearly fifty years, the US Army Air Force Hospital at Morley had been rotting in a Norfolk field. The Americans had come as the largest invasion of England since the Danes, about a hundred thousand men, half of whom were in the Eighth Air Force heavy bomber units in East Anglia. The Second Air Division with their B24 Liberators and the Third Air Division with their B19 Flying Fortress planes flew daylight raids from eighteen bases within thirty miles of Norwich to bomb Nazi Germany. Very many of them died. Many are buried in the American Cemetery at Madingley near Cambridge. Of those who were wounded, if they made it alive to Morley Hospital, 96% survived.

After the Americans left, their hospital wards became the dormitories and class-rooms of an Emergency Teacher Training College. Then in 1951, the visionary County Education Officer, Lincoln Ralphs, persuaded Norfolk to buy the 1000 bed hospital site and to use it as a technical grammar boarding school for children from all over the rural County. By this imaginative scheme, Norfolk was one of the few Counties to set up technical grammar school provision under the 1944 Act for the whole of Norfolk.

Sir Lincoln, as he later became, also provided the new College with a motto, a prayer and a song which is still sung. Deep in the DNA of Wymondham College are the themes of truth conquering tyranny, of triumph in overcoming adversity, and of wisdom flourishing. Knowledge, faith and courtesy became the shared value of a community which lives, plays and works together.

Little of this heritage was known to me when I received that 'phone call in early 1992. Ron Wolsey told me that he planned to retire after twenty one years at the College and the Governors were looking for his successor.

'Was I interested?'

I had not applied, but was persuaded along with other State Boarding School Heads to visit the school with our wives to meet the Governors.

My first impression was one of utter amazement, that a school which seemed to celebrate dereliction could continue to convince loving parents that their 11 year old children would be well looked after and flourish in such depressing surroundings.

It was clear that Wymondham College had had a distinguished past – it had once been the largest and most successful Grammar School in England – but what of the future? The school was now comprehensive. The boarding numbers had been falling for some years. Recruitment of girls at 11 was particularly challenging. Norfolk had tried to close the College in 1986 and it was only saved by the herculean efforts of Governors, parents and even the pupils in raising just enough money to attend to the most urgent needs.

I met with the Governors who were a wonderful team of the great and the good of Norfolk, amongst them one Lord and two Ladies, one Marshall of the Royal Air Force, one Air Vice-Marshall, one Lieutenant Colonel, a leading light of the Political Party who controlled the County Council, several successful businessmen and farmers, and two parents. I gave them my honest view about the College's future.

'*You need ten million pounds of capital spending and ten years, then, if it has survived, you will have a viable school.*'

We went back to Louth, not at all sure that even if the Governors were interested in employing someone who had been so frank and so rude about their school, we would want to accept the job. The Chairman 'phoned next day and asked me to take it on. We moved to Norfolk.

9. Survival

'….a school which seemed to celebrate dereliction….'

Moving to Norfolk in 1992 was hard for my wife, Jenny. Our eldest son left school that summer and went off to University. Our younger son became a boarder so we became boarding parents and the occupants of two homes, our house in Louth for use in school holidays and boarders' leave weekends, and the College Principal's house.

Jenny missed having the boys at home and her Louth friends. She was not impressed when we had to take out a bank loan to furnish the College house, all for the privilege of living next to the best collection of rusting Nissen huts in Western Europe. When the Governors laid on a staff function to welcome 'the New Principal and his Wife', we invited all the College employees. The teachers believed that they were 'the staff'. My view was that all those adults who worked on the College campus and were therefore in contact with our pupils were my colleagues on the staff. Matrons, catering staff, the maintenance team, even the grounds men, all were invited to the party.

I shall never forget the thanks I got from one of the College gardeners. He told me with tears in his eyes that he had worked for more than twenty years at the College and never before had anyone told him that he was a member of staff. And yet all the adults working at a boarding school have a role to play. Pupils who are unhappy or disgruntled are more likely to confide in a matron than a teacher, and may well find it easier to talk to an un-threatening grounds man weeding a border than to their House Tutor.

Pulling together as a team was a start, but we still had to convince parents that they should leave their children in our care. The place looked so depressing. I discussed what might be done in the short term with Clive, the Vice Principal in charge of everything that did not involve teachers or pupils, i.e. buildings, finance, catering, grounds, even the sewage farm that I discovered I was now responsible for. We agreed that if the huts were at least painted green, to blend in with our attractive lawns, rather than a rusty red, they might look less derelict.

My own office was at the end of what was known as the 'Admin Hut'. Parents coming to see me had to walk through a succession of bays with accounts staff, secretaries, deputies, catering managers all interested in who was coming to see me. Sometimes these parents were struggling with the boarding fees or their son or daughter was in trouble. They hated having to walk through the office staff on the way to me.

My actual office had two doors, one at the end of the admin corridor and the other a fire escape door in the end wall of the hut. One afternoon during my first term in Norfolk, after a particularly distressing meeting with a mother who despaired of her son ever surviving at the

119

College, let alone passing his exams, I decided to spare her the ordeal of a return trip through all the admin staff.

'Come out this way,' I suggested, grasping the handle of the fire escape door and pushing hard.

To my and her amazement, the door, complete with timber frame, fell out of the end wall of the hut and landed with a crunch on the concrete path outside. She burst into giggles at the sight of the Principal still holding the door handle. It was the best thing that had happened to her all day.

But for me it was the final straw – the Admin Hut had to go and I had to find a new home from which to run the school. Fortunately, with the retirement of a Vice Principal a flat became vacant in the ground floor of a boarding house. The boarding houses were by far the most respectable parts of the College and one house, which was then used for 6th Form boarders, had already been partially converted for teaching use. I set up my office in the vacant flat, with an office for my secretary next door. Just next to both of us, there was a large space for a staff room. The Building even had an entrance hall which could be adapted as a reception office. The admin hut was not just closed. It was demolished. All the admin staff moved in to our new base.

~

If Jenny and I were struggling to settle into our new community, we appreciated that it would be far more difficult for our new 11 year old pupils. Leaving home for the first time and becoming a boarder at school is hard, for the children and for their parents. At the College, I was told, the House staff found that it was best to encourage the parents to drop their children off at the House and then leave them to get on with meeting each other in their new surroundings without extended and inevitably tearful farewells. There was then a get-together for parents over a stiffening glass of wine and something to eat to encourage them to get to know each other and to meet senior staff, before setting off for home.

Perhaps because the girls are much more mature than the boys at eleven, they would settle better and generally fall asleep after the initial excitement of the first evening in the House had worn off. Some of the boys would suffer from very real home sickness and, for them, drastic strategies sometimes helped. At the College we had a boarding house colleague whose approach involved singing and a love of football. Boys who were homesick and tearful would not be left to cry themselves to sleep but told to get their dressing gowns on and report to the Day Room downstairs which had a piano. There they would be given a drink and biscuit and instructed to sing as loudly as they could. It always started with '*I'm for ever blowing bubbles*' as the teacher was a West Ham fan, but then they would go through the whole repertoire of football songs. '*You'll never walk alone*', '*Glory, Glory Leeds United*', '*Keep the Blue flag flying here*', '*When the Spurs go marching in*', until very tired and hoarse boys would plead to go back to bed. It worked, partly because the same boys joined his Under 12 Football team and the College Boys' Choir, united in a shared experience of triumph over adversity.

But the real problem was not just initial home-sickness, it was that boarding numbers at the College were falling. Fewer and fewer Y7 girls and to a lesser extent boys, were joining the 11-16 Main School Houses. At the same time, 6th Form boarding was relatively stable. Nearly all those who completed Year 11 stayed into Year 12. The challenge was to make the College more attractive to parents of 11 year olds while encouraging 16 year olds to stay, with a particular focus on attracting and retaining girls.

We all knew that 16 year old girls did better at GCSE than 16 year old boys. Having a majority of boys in Y11 was therefore going to have a depressing effect on our examination results. That was most clearly shown in 1993, when the Y11 ratio for boys to girls was just under two. As we were able to attract more girls, the ratio came down until it reached about 1.3 and remained steady at that. In a world where examination results are the most vital measure of a school's success, a ratio of 2:1 girls to boys would do wonders for any school even if the strength of the boys' Rugby XVs might not be so impressive!

I knew that some schools, including Old Swinford, had set up 'junior houses' specifically for 11, or 11 and 12 year olds, so that they could settle into a new school in a relatively protective environment before facing the pressure of being with a large number of older pupils day and night. I thought that we needed such a 'junior house', but the only possible way of achieving this was to switch one of the two houses used for the 6th Form boarding back to being exclusively for younger children.

As it happened, there was another reason why I thought that this would be of benefit. The College had a very strong male rugby-playing culture with many very good features. But there was one less attractive one, especially to those 6th Form girls who had to move across from their boarding house to take their meals in the other 6th Form house. The young men of the 1st XV had got into the habit of sitting in the common room waiting for their evening meal and enjoying watching the girls coming through. I don't think that they intended to be either threatening or provocative but the girls found it embarrassing, especially as the boys were not above making comparative comments about each girl as she passed.

I met with all the staff Heads of House to discuss our options. We did not have the millions of pounds which it would cost to build another boarding house, but we could accommodate all the Y13 (U6th) boarders in the House with the dining room. We could make the four 'Main School' houses run from year 8 to year 12, and admit all the new Y7 pupils, boys and girls into the House vacated by the 6th Formers.

The Main School House Heads were anxious about this plan, not least because they liked to give their Y11 boarders key roles of responsibility in their Houses. Moving the population up a year would mean having to adjust to having 6th Formers staying with them. They also regretting losing their Y7s as they valued the chance to 'break them in' as members of their house communities, but they could see that our boarding numbers were falling. Something needed to be done.

The alterations needed to set up the Y7 house, Peel, were minimal. A strong team of staff as Head of House, Deputy Head, Tutors and Matrons was recruited for the new arrangements, all from existing staff. With re-decorated dormitories, bright new duvets and a focus on what would help 11 year olds to settle in, the feed-back from parents applying for places at the College was very positive. The new House started with most of the beds filled and both boarding and day Y7s sharing the Common Rooms on the ground floor. They still went to lessons all around the College and had their meals with their 'parent' houses in the

College refectory, but for break-time, lunch-time and after school, their lives were based in Peel.

The changes in the other Houses were more slowly accepted but eventually staff and students got used to the new arrangements. Having older students living in the Main School houses provided more leadership, although the Year 11 students were initially upset at being bossed about by the L6th. The most important change was that, very slowly, our boarding number began to creep up and the College future began to look more secure.

~

With my office in the ground floor of Peel Hall, my own contact with Y7 was dramatically increased. I decided that I would try to teach every Y7, Y10 and Y13 pupil. My teaching subject was chemistry but the Science Department were not keen to have a teacher contributing to their exam results who was all too frequently called away to meeting and crises. I had to teach something else. It was agreed that I would teach a module of the Y7 Religious Studies course for each Tutor Group in turn. RS was my second subject.

The Y10 Health Education module enabled me to teach all of that year group in turn and an hour each week of contribution to the A level General Studies programme gave me contact with Y13. This pattern enabled me to say to the parents that I did actually teach all their children over a two year cycle, and to say to the staff that I knew the problems they faced with the most challenging pupils because I had met them all in my teaching groups. I had the same problems with them as we all did.

The other area where Jenny and I felt that we could make a contribution to the College's support for Year 7 was at weekends. Many of our boarders went home on Saturdays after games in the afternoon and returned on Monday morning but many stayed. Sundays could seem very long for the eleven year olds far from home. Jenny opened our kitchen at home to small groups of both girls and boys for a 'Cookery Club'. This kept groups of up to ten children happily making chocolate crack-o-lates, peppermint drops or cupcakes after Sunday lunch.

My own activities with the Y7 boarders tended to involve gardening, often with the devoted member of staff who ran the Gardening Club, working on a small patch of the College grounds or in a greenhouse to produce potted plants, fruit and vegetables which they could then sell to visiting parents or at the College Summer Fayre.

The College has an eighty three acre site including wide areas of grass, a large wood and very many sports pitches. The grounds staff preferred to maintain this as a municipal park rather than something softer and more welcoming. I spent time talking to them and the boarders on how we could make it more attractive. At the centre of the campus was a large but not deep pond, with rushes and willow trees, the favourite haunt of mallards. The gently sloping banks were good places in the summer to sit and read a book or talk to your friends.

For seven autumns, on my way home to Louth from the College for a leave weekend, I stopped just outside King's Lynn to buy a sack of daffodil bulbs. They were not expensive if you bought 50 kgs of one variety and each autumn I took these bulbs back with me to the College. If there was a sunny Sunday around October, I took a collection of forks and the sack of bulbs down to the grass by the College pond and with the help of a team of Y7 pupils from Peel, planted all the bulbs in a large patch. The grounds staff were sceptical.

'Waste of time planting daffodils – the kids'll just pick the lot.'

But they never did. Each year group had their own large patch of colour in the spring, a riot of daffodils spreading year by year in different varieties at slightly different flowering times around our College pond. Each year the pupils who had planted them would come and admire each other's collection and as the ring of glorious colour crept around the pond, they began to be noticed, admired and nurtured by everyone.

'..a riot of daffodils spreading year by year in different varieties at slightly different flowering times around our College pond..'

If any visiting younger brother or sister ever picked a daffodil, they soon learnt not to do it again. When the flowers had died, I had to persuade the grounds staff to leave them until June to die off before they ran the big mowers over the brown remains, but the College daffodils gave a lot of pleasure to the pupils and their parents

'We planted those,' they would tell their Mums and Dads when they came to pick them up for leave weekends. 'Aren't they lovely?'

~

One spring afternoon, there was a commotion outside my office door. Tearing myself away from the latest gripping Government Circular on a scheme for changes to Age Weighted Pupil Unit allocation in three year school budgets, I quietly opened the door. Two excited twelve year olds were jumping up and down in the adjacent Secretary's Office.

'They're drowning, you've got to help!' spluttered the less distraught girl, her friend sobbing beside her.

The look of horror on the Secretary's face told me what she was thinking. The dire warnings of the County Health and Safety Officer that we should put a ten foot fence around the pond at the centre of the College site had come all too true. We had failed to put up the fence, not wanting to turn an attractive feature into a section of a prison camp. Now, someone was drowning.

'Call an ambulance," I shouted as I sprinted out of the door, with the girls in hot pursuit. 'Which part of the pond are they in, this side or the other?'

One quick look told me that no-one was anywhere near the pond. It seemed completely peaceful and deserted.

'Over here, Sir,' the girls shouted together. 'They're drowning over here!'

A small group of boarders stood by the house wall, looking anxiously into an open drain. They had pulled off the cover and left it lying on the grass. 'They've got stuck and can't get out. We heard them crying but we can't reach them. You've got longer arms, Sir. You'll be able to save them if you're quick.'

And then the penny dropped. It was the duckling season. Enterprising ducks made their nests on the flat roofed extension of the boarding-house day room safe from the school cats, whose kittens caused almost as much excitement amongst the youngest boarders. Come hatching time, the ducklings limbered up for a life of swimming and flying by pottering across the flat roof. When the duck flew off the roof to reach the pond, the ducklings threw themselves into space and like fluffy parachutists sailed down after her, none the worse for their adventure.

But that day it had rained, very hard. The water caught the last two of a brood of roof-hatched ducklings on their way to the edge of the roof, washed them into the gutter and flushed them down the drain-pipe into the drain, where they were still swimming for dear life and cheeping pathetically.

'Hang on!" I said, either to the ducks or the children. 'Let me get my jacket off, and I'll try to fish them out.'

Which explains why two puzzled parents visiting the school were told by the member of staff showing them round that the man in a suit, on his knees in the garden with his arm down a drain while surrounded by excited children was, in fact, the Principal. He was a little busy just now but would be delighted to meet them in a while!

~

For the girls, boredom rather than home sickness was sometimes the problem. Few ever really wanted to run away from school, either in Louth or in Wymondham, but on warm and summer evenings we had occasional 'Midnight Runners' in both schools. Just before the Half-term holiday one Summer Term in Louth, the weather was warm enough for the first barbecue of the year in our garden. As the sun went down, the full moon bathed the fields around the

128

school in an eyrie light. Just before midnight, we decided to move indoors before the insects spoiled the evening. Then the 'phone rang.

''ello. Is that the 'eadmaster?' a gruff voice said.

'This is Mr Haden, how can I help you?'

'We've got two of your lasses here, the wife and me. They're having a cup of tea in our kitchen. They're none the worse for wear but they said I should 'phone you and tell you that they weren't in bed in t' school. Can you come for 'em?'

'I'll come right away. Where do you live?'

It was about six miles from the school to the farm, down the back road through the rich arable area to the south. The caller's directions took me off the road and down a long grassy drive until a white painted farmhouse appeared. Even in the moonlight, the farm was surrounded by fields of the deep yellows and greens of maturing crops. I knocked on the door.

'Come in,' said the round smiling farmer's wife who appeared at the door. 'They're in 'ere.'

And there they were, two Y8 twelve-year olds, sipping their tea as if it was perfectly normal for the Principal to collect them after a long country walk in the middle of the night. I thanked the farmer and his wife for their kindness and told the girls to get in my car. On the way back to school, they told me what had happened. They were bored, they said. It was a hot night and they couldn't sleep, so about an hour after the staff had checked that they were safe in bed at their Lights Out, they decided to go for a walk.

'We weren't really running away from school', they said. 'We were just looking for an adventure. Lucy's aunty lives not far away so we decided to give her a nice surprise.'

They had been there before and were sure they could find the place once they had set off in the right direction. They knew it was south of the school. So they waited until all the seniors and staff were in Prep, put on track suits over their pyjamas, tip-toed out of their dormitory carrying their trainers and slipped out of the House. As good Girl Guides, they knew which way south was and set off down the back-roads, enjoying the warmth of the evening and their new-found freedom. No-one passed them on the road, no-one to stop and enquire what two girls in track suits were doing wandering around late at night.

About a mile from the school, they found the bridleway which leads south through the fields.

'It was a lovely walk,' said one of them brightly, 'but after a bit, Lucy started wheezing. She'd left her inhaler behind and her asthma was getting really bad.'

'I think it was those yellow flowers in the fields that did it,' said Lucy. 'So we thought we'd better get some help. That's when we found the farm. Mr and Mrs Riggall were ever so kind.'

By that time we were almost back at the boarding house and I realised that in my haste I had completely forgotten to let the staff know that two of their girls were missing. We drove up to the silent house and quietly got out of the car.

'What are you going to tell our parents?' said Lucy. 'They'll be hopping mad that we went out on our own.'

As both of them were fine and had not really intended to run away, I decided to play down the escapade provided that both girls on their Guide's honour promised never to do such a silly thing again.

'Let's sort that out in the morning. But whatever you do, don't tell your mothers what you said to me in the car.' They looked puzzled, and then the penny dropped. 'Oh you mean when I said there was a lot of rape about,' said Lucy grinning.

'That's it,' I said. 'And now get back to bed the pair of you.'

~

Gradually, the numbers of parents applying for places at the College for their 11 year old sons and daughters crept up as Peel Hall became increasingly popular for both day and boarding parents. For parents wanting a day place, we had to ensure that acceptable criteria could be applied within the national admissions framework as parents clearly wanted access to the excellent sport, music and drama which the College offered but which was funded and staffed from our boarding tradition and fee income. We somehow had to control day entry by having a strict limit on day places and ring-fencing boarding places to ensure no erosion to day status.

Pupils who were admitted as boarders were not allowed to transfer to day. Day pupil applications were restricted to within an increasingly small 'proximity' ring around the College and we had many discussions as to where the proximity measurement started from and finished at. Our College land covered a wide area and some parents living on one side could claim to be nearer the nearest College tree or blade of grass to those living on the other side. In the end we defined 'the College' as centred on my office desk and the proximity was 'as the crow flies' from the parent's home defined as the point at which they left their own house to access the nearest public road. Every Admissions Appeals season, there would be much pouring over large scale maps before the Governors' decisions were accepted as reasonable and fair.

Many day parents wanted their sons and daughters to be able to take full advantage of all our activities and we decided to allow this for 'day-boarders', pupils who could join their House before breakfast from 7.30 am and stay until after Prep around 8 pm, provided that they paid a fee to cover the cost of facilities and staffing. Such parents had no priority for day places but once offered a place could opt for 'day-boarding'. Fortunately, this arrangement has survived all the discussions of 'fair admissions' since the mid-1990s.

As the numbers of applications rose, so did the test-scores of those who were admitted to Year 7. In effect, we were not 'selecting' pupils, their parents were selecting us. As the only state school in Norfolk which had places open to all families across the County, and in fact across England and even abroad, we had no 'catchment area' and the County Council had no responsibility for transporting pupils to our doors. Parents had to choose and parents had either to pay for a boarding place or get their children here daily. For some families, our insistence that all pupils attend school on Saturday morning and the fact that our school day was longer than most day schools were disincentives, but most families were keen to get a place, either day if they lived near enough, or boarding if they were happy with that option and could pay for it.

Every September, we tested all the new Y7 pupils using Cognitive Ability Tests (CAT) which gave two numbers, one for verbal reasoning and one for non-verbal reasoning. They were internationally recognised tests and as 'culture free' as any other we could find. They gave both a useful assessment for setting in mathematics and modern languages after the first term, and a measure of the relative overall ability of the year group. The best and simplest measure of this was the ratio of the number of children in Y7 with scores above 100 (the average ability child) to below 100. If we rolled forward these ratios to Year 11 we knew that in 1992, this ratio would still be 5:1 but that it would steadily fall so that by 1996, our Y11 would have a ratio of 3:1 and if our intake did not improve it would continue to fall to close to 1.0. In simple terms, it would become harder and harder to maintain the excellent results on which the College's academic reputation was based as the educational potential of our Year 7 had been going down year by year.

Our Y11 and A level results were already well above the national average and they hovered around the 65% of Y11 achieving five or more GCSE A-C passes for each year from 1992 to 1994. As this was against a declining ratio of more to less able students, this was a huge achievement by the teaching staff. Confidence in the College was maintained and with the establishment of Peel as our Y7 house, the ratio of more able to less able pupils began to increase. By 1994, it had increased to 6.3 and by 1995, to 8.1. Parents were choosing us as a good school to care for and educate their children. With these improved Y7 scores, we could expect our GCSE results to steadily get better. Year by year they did. When the measurement of Value Added (VA) came in with national Y6 SAT scores compared with our Y9 SAT scores and our Y11 GCSE results, our College VA results showed that, not only were our results improving in absolute terms, our VA scores showed that the pupils had done even better than their increased ability had suggested.

Although, in 1992, the College was no longer under the control of the Norfolk Education Authority, we still had the support of the Norfolk County Council's scheme for assisted boarding places. At the time I joined the College, there were almost a hundred boarders supported by grants from the County budget, about 20% of our boarding places. These places were awarded not on academic or any other merit but on 'boarding need'.

By the time we left the College in 2000, the numbers of boarders supported by Norfolk or any other Local Authority had dwindled to almost zero. The pressure on Local Authority budgets and the opposition within Social Service departments to the option of placing children with difficult home circumstances in boarding places was cutting off pupils with a boarding need from the College. Their social workers preferred to find foster care for most children and places in Children's Homes for those most difficult to place. Only now, when the national concern about improving the very poor educational outcomes for 'looked after children' has become a priority, has the state and independent boarding school option come to the forefront of Local Authority thinking. Norfolk is again a pioneer of new schemes to help 'cared for' children with Assisted Boarding places.

So who were our Y7 boarders, where did they come from and why were they with us? Many were from relatively affluent Norfolk families who knew about the College's strong reputation and wanted their children to have the opportunity that they may themselves have had. Significant proportions were the children of former pupils or had heard about the College from former pupils. Norfolk still had some active RAF stations and once had very many more. RAF families from Coltishall or Marham would hear about our boarding places and want their children to join us, often after completing their primary schooling at the state primary school nearest to the RAF base.

As the MOD began to shut down RAF stations in Norfolk, RAF Coltishall finally closed in 2006, other MOD families in Suffolk and Cambridgeshire, where there were no State Boarding options, came to our door. The Army Air Corps at Wattisham in Suffolk and the Royal Anglians at Colchester also had families with children at Wymondham supported by MOD boarding grants. The Royal Lancers moved into the former RAF Swanton Morley and we developed good links with their Sergeants Mess, which helped to generate boarding applications.

Other families who would have in the past sent their sons and daughters as boarders to Gresham's School in Holt or Langley School near Norfolk were finding it increasingly difficult to meet the cost of the escalating fees. They began to consider the College as a serious alternative. We occasionally lost girls who found our large, mixed and comprehensive boarding community too complicated to the much smaller all–girls community of Hethersett Old Hall School. Most of our girls liked the mixed company and their parents valued the fact that brothers and sisters could go to the same school. More and more families began to look seriously at the College as a good alternative to the independent sector.

Our junior dormitories in all the Houses were six-bed units, six boys or six girls, often coming to us from very different backgrounds. In one group of six girls in Peel in the Autumn Term 1994, you might find the daughter of a farming family from a Norfolk village, the daughter of a military Officer posted overseas, the daughter of a single parent with a terminal illness whose grandmother had care of her, the daughter of a regional businesswoman, the daughter of a serviceman in the Army Air Corps and the daughter of a Suffolk vicar. In his speech at his last College Prize Giving, the former Principal of Wymondham, Melvyn Roffe said:

'.....*students here know that people come in all kinds each with their own story; that not everyone can be your best friend but it is possible to respect even those you don't much like; that there is no limit on aspiration other than that which you place on aspiration yourself.*'

He was right and our six eleven year old girls in a Peel A Dorm would have the opportunity to learn that lesson over the next seven years of their College life. We should give these girls, part of our Y7 intake in 1994, their names.

Julia's Dad had been at an independent school as a boy and had sent his two sons there, but the farm had not been doing well and the cost of a third child in independent boarding was going to be just too much. His youngest son had played for his school U16 Rugby XV when they met Wymondham in the County Cup Final, and had lost. Julia's Dad was impressed by the fact that a state school had beaten the independent school which took pride in producing the County's best Rugby players. When they come to the College and discovered that we had a swimming pool and an AstroTurf hockey pitch, Julia was keen to come to us. She just loved all sports, a bubbly girl of about average intelligence who had lots of friends in her village Primary School – the report her Head sent in to support her application to us suggested that she would really enjoy being a boarder, and she did.

Hannah's Mum came with her when she came for a boarding interview with me and I had the clear impression that we may be interviewing her daughter, but Mrs H-J, wife of Group Captain H-J, came to interview me. As the daughter of a serving officer, Hannah could board at any school, even the most expensive. Hannah and her mother were planning to visit an Essex Catholic girls' school after visiting us. While I met her mother, Hannah told the member of staff interviewing her that she really wanted to go to a mixed school. She also said that she hated boarding at the Prep School where her parents had left her from the age of six when they went off to Saudi Arabia with her Dad's new job. But boarding with us 'would be alright because Granny lives in Norwich and has promised to have me for weekends'. We were pleased to hear that Mrs H-J would like to go through with her application – I must have passed the interview!

Anna was already being supported by her Grandmother. Her father had left the family just after Anna was born and her mother had been diagnosed with cancer when Anna was nine. She was now eleven and the doctors had given her mother just a few more months to live. Anna and her mother moved into her Granny's small terrace house and it was her Granny who had applied for a boarding place. She was planning to pay Anna's boarding fees out of the money that her father still paid for her maintenance under a Court Order but sometimes, the money did not arrive and it took so long for the court to track down the father and get him to pay that Granny was worried that Anna might lose her boarding place.

So she applied to Norfolk County Council for a boarding grant and they said that they would help if we offered Ann a boarding place. She was interviewed and we were worried about her. Her clothes were incredibly old fashioned, a long skirt her Granny had made for her and a knitted jumper that seemed shapeless. She said that she enjoyed reading. Her

137

school report described her as an introverted little girl sometimes bullied by the other Y6 pupils in her Primary School but of about average ability. Her one virtue seemed to be that she tried to get on with everyone but did not make friends easily.

Jane's Mum ran an agency business, hiring out theatre costumes to Amateur Dramatic Groups and small Theatres all over East Anglia. She was often away overnight and although her Dad was good at looking after her, he worked in London, commuting by train from Norwich. They had been to a College production of Nicholas Nickleby and had decided that Jane would love boarding with us. Fortunately, Jane thought she might like to come too and was looking forward to taking part in as much drama, in class and in school shows as possible. We were sure that she would also provide lots of personal drama as she settled in but on balance thought that she would cope.

The Army Air Corps moved into their Wattisham base in 1992 just after we came to Wymondham, having come back from German as part of the MOD Draw-Down changes. They flew Lynx helicopters and were unusual in that NCOs, Sergeants and Corporals in the Corps, flew helicopters. In the RAF, all the pilots were commissioned officers by 1996 although Sergeant Pilots had flown in WWII. Mary's Dad was one of these AAC pilots and had already served tours of duty in Iraq and was now training to deploy to Bosnia. Her Mum was keen to get her settled in boarding before her Dad had to go away again. We thought that she would be fine, although it would be hard for her, worrying about her Dad.

Finally, there was Iris, the Vicar's daughter. Her mother had been one of the first women to be ordained priest at Easter 1994 and had been appointed to a post in large rural

Suffolk parish. Iris lived with her Mum and her Dad, two much older sisters, two dogs and numerous chickens in the village vicarage. There were no other children nearby of her age and she was lonely. Her Mum had come to a Remembrance Day Service in our College Chapel and had talked to our Chaplain about Sunday services for boarders and daily Chapel Assemblies. She told me after Iris joined us that what she liked about us was the way that we welcomed pupils of all Christian denominations and in fact all faiths or none, but when they arrived at the College all our boarders were encouraged to take spiritual realities seriously.

Six A Dorm borders in Peel, sleeping together whether they liked it or not, required as boarders to help each other to cope with being away from home and facing new challenges and new opportunities as they settled in to the College.

10. Fit for Learning and Living?

Wymondham College's new Technology building: '…..from one side, the new building looked magnificent, bold, white and modern…..'

In 1584, Archdeacon Robert Johnson of North Luffenham in Rutland decided to use his wealth from multiple parishes to endow two new grammar schools for the boys of Oakham and Uppingham towns. He ensured that his schools had buildings which would last. Their stone schoolrooms still stand near to the parish church of each town and are still used by the boarding schools that grew out of Johnson's charitable provision for the local communities.

At Uppingham, from Edward Thring's time onwards, the school expanded as more boarding houses were opened around the centre of the town. These houses are the heart of the school today, fifteen residential communities for boys and for girls where the staff and their families live, eat and work alongside the boarders. The school remains one of England's leading independent boarding schools with a very fine academic record.

In Oakham, Johnson's school remained the day grammar school for the town with a relatively small number of boys for hundreds of years. In 1910, it became a day Direct Grant grammar school serving Oakham and Rutland while continuing to admit fee-paying boarders. When the Direct Grant was withdrawn in 1970, the Headmaster at the time took the school into the independent sector and the school also admitted girls. In the 1970s, the school received significant funds from the family trust of John Jerwood MC, on Old Boy of the school. He made a fortune from pearl trading in the Far East and gifts to the school enabled Oakham to expand and to build new boarding accommodation. 'Jerwoods', the Lower School section of the school, was named in his honour. The school uses a worship book of prayers, psalms and hymns which includes special services for 'Jerwoods Family Harvest' and 'Jerwoods Morning Prayer'.

Both Uppingham and Oakham have superb modern teaching facilities alongside their comfortable boarding houses and are very successful schools today. Other independent boarding schools are housed in even more palatial buildings. Eton College still uses the fine Tudor buildings of its original foundation.

In the early 1990s, Wymondham College's Nissen huts looked slightly better having been painted green. But nothing could really disguise the fact that 70% of all our teaching accommodation was still housed in wartime corrugated iron. Between 1988 and 1992, the boarding roll had declined from about 720 to about 580, leaving 140 boarding beds unoccupied. At 1992 boarding fee levels, this meant an annual loss of income to the College of about £450,000 and a cumulative loss over five years of over £1.5 million. If these beds could be filled, the boarding fee income could be invested in improving the College.

In 1992, the College seemed almost to celebrate the dereliction of the huts. It was not just a matter of how they looked; what they cost in terms of heating bills and unoccupied space was also crippling the College budget. According to the DfE's most recent survey (Feb 1989), the College had a teaching capacity of 1483 places, most of it in under-used Nissen Huts. The College put in bids for capital funding for new buildings in 1991 and 1992. Both bids had failed. The DfE could reasonably argue that we had so much teaching space that more would be a luxury. If we were ever to replace the huts, we had to reduce our 'nominal capacity' and emphasise the financial burden of maintaining and heating fifty year old corrugated iron huts.

We first negotiated an agreement with the DfE that our capacity on paper would be reduced to 1180 with only 356 places in permanent buildings. The only way to persuade staff that they did not need small 6th form teaching spaces at the ends of our huts, some of which were only used for 20% of the teaching week but heated from dawn to dusk in winter, was to demolish the whole hut! With the annual heating bill for the College running at about £250,000, we were simply providing Norfolk's flocks of wood-pigeons with wonderfully warm places on which to roost! Somehow we had to get the huts replaced.

Fortunately, the DfE was looking for schools to develop a Specialist curriculum, with a particular interest in Design and Technology. If we could find commercial sponsorship to raise £150,000 we could be awarded Specialist School status with an enhanced revenue budget and access to capital funds for improving teaching facilities.

Lotus Cars had their manufacturing and research base at Hethel just outside Wymondham and Tony Rudd, one of their Directors, had become a College Governor. He persuaded the Lotus Board to support us with a gift of a car a year over three years. The Company was short of cash but had a stock of cars. The first was a second-hand Lotus Carlton, a very fast version of the Vauxhall family car. It had left-hand-drive and made very impressive engine noises. I was terrified that one of the 6th Form would borrow it for a practice run around our athletics track but we managed to sell it as rapidly as possible and put the money into the sponsorship fund.

The College Technology department, led by Alan Booth, was already establishing a reputation for excellence in design projects when we decided to bid for capital funds for a new building. We wanted something which made a statement about the national importance of Design and Technology and reflected the College origins as Norfolk's only Technical Grammar School. The Governors were keen to recruit a gifted architect to turn our vision into reality. They ran a competitive bid process which brought Paul Tanner, of Trevlyn Tanner Architects, into our development team.

Paul drew up an ambitious plan for a Design and Technology Centre to form the centre-piece of the College site. The building was to be cruciform in shape and should encourage an integrated Design and Technology curriculum. A large central atrium and resource area led off into facilities for Multi-material Technology, IT and Control Technology, Food Technology, Design, Sculpture and Graphics. The model of the finished structure looked wonderful. The only problem was that the estimated overall cost was about £3.3 million, which we did not have.

What we did have was a collection of war-time temporary buildings, roasting hot in summer and impossible to heat in winter. They sat on a network of war-time sewers which were infested with rats. When the rats got cold, they came up into the classrooms to join the College's pupils. We also had in Clive Richardson an expert in writing capital bids supported by photographs of rusting iron, cold pupils and dead rats. He even claimed that a live rat appeared in one image.

The Funding Agency for Schools made sympathetic noises and awarded an initial grant of £700,000 as we were part of the Technology Schools Initiative. The College raised a further £250,000 from commercial sponsorship and our own business activities, so we were well on our way towards the first £1 million. We had warned Paul that his fine building might have to be completed in Phases and he had designed it to be capable of construction in two self-sufficient halves.

Phase 1 of the 'Technology Block' was opened in 1994 by Rt Hon John McGregor, Former Secretary of State for Education and Transport Secretary at the time. From one side, the new building looked magnificent, bold, white and modern. From the other, it looked very odd with a massive timber and glass screen slicing the structure in half and a very large empty space where the rest, we hoped, would be.

The next stage was to move all Modern Languages teaching from their Nissen huts into the HORSA buildings vacated by Design and Technology. This was accepted as less than ideal, from one group of wartime temporary huts to

144

another, but at least the Languages teachers could work in concrete rather than corrugated iron and be much nearer to the heart of the teaching area.

In the summer of 1996, Cheryl Gillan MP, Under-Secretary of State for Education, came to visit Peel Hall and to present College awards to students. We showed her the first half of the Technology Building and the space where the second half might be. In the following year, the College was at last awarded a grant to start the building this second half to complete the structure. The regional paper, the Eastern Daily Press (EDP) published a cartoon showing two curved teachers in a hutted classroom saying

'....the bad news is that Mrs Tablock and I will have to retire, children. After many years of teaching in Nissen huts we're the wrong shape for normal classrooms!'

It took us a further year to complete the job, with the opening of the second Phase of the Technology Building by Charles Clarke MP, Under Secretary of State for Education, and MP for Norwich South. This brought Art, Business Studies, Geography and Learning Support in from the cold Nissen huts.

Lotus Cars continued to support us and a message came to say 'why haven't you collected your new car?'

To my amazed delight I learnt that the Lotus board, thanks to Tony Rudd's persuasive powers, had agreed to give us a brand new Lotus Elise. I drove this bright yellow sports car very cautiously back down the A11 to the College, being overtaken by articulated juggernauts whose wheel nuts seemed to me to be about the same level as my head. At the next Saturday Assembly, Alison Scott, complete with WW1 leather flying helmet and goggles drove the car into the Sport Hall. I handed over the keys of the Lotus to one of our new

Y7 boarders whose name just happened to be Eloise. She stepped elegantly into the car and handed the keys to Alison. They drove out of the Assembly with a roaring engine and over a thousand cheering voices ringing in their ears. We sold the brand new car as soon as possible and had another £23,000 to add to the building fund.

With the building of another two Science laboratories, the moving of Mathematics into space vacated by Science and my insistence that all teaching space should be in timetabled use for a minimum of 75% of the teaching week, we could finally plan to clear the whole front of the College of all traces of World War II temporaries. Just English, Religious studies and History remained in huts.

History actually quite liked being the last to move. They felt that teaching in WII temporaries added to their credibility. In 1998, the College bid for new English and Humanities classrooms was successful. In November of the following year, Sir Peter Hall performed the formal opening of the new Humanities and English building complete with Drama Studio and gave a master-class to the cast of our College production of Romeo and Juliet.

At last, the College had a set of buildings fit both to live in and to learn in. Just one Nissen hut was preserved. The College Chapel which had been a hospital ward in 1943-5, remained as a place for daily and Sunday worship. It is a fitting reminder to us all of the sacrifices of all the young men who had come from America to fight for freedom from oppression and to learn to triumph over adversity, fear, freezing cold and being shot at, while at 30,000 feet over Nazi Germany.

The small mortuary which had been used for those few US Airmen patients who did not survive their wounds was partially demolished and then rebuilt to form a memorial garden. It served as a memorial to all those who had died in the 2nd Air Division, USAAF, during the 1940s. The work was done by College teaching staff and students working with a group of Ugandan students and their Head and teachers. They had come to Wymondham for a month to return our visit two years before, to their school in Arua, Uganda, the same school in West Nile where Jenny and I had taught thirty years before. The garden made another attractive place for young people to sit and enjoy the sun in a busy and demanding community.

With the new buildings and improving examination results, the College was on the way to re-establishing itself as a very successful school. Boarding numbers were climbing again. Day places were now increasingly offered as 'day-boarding' as that was what parents wanted.

Over the first fifteen years of the 21st Century, the College continued to attract major capital funding for both boarding and teaching. A large new 6th Form boarding extension to Lincoln Hall has provided the space to accommodate all 6th Form boarders with all U6th Y13 students in en-suite study bedrooms *more like a university college than a school building*. The new development, called the Lincoln Ralphs Building, provides comfortable single and twin-bedded accommodation for all 16-19 students in term-time and a very valuable facility to generate letting income for conferences in the school holidays.

With boarding waiting lists getting longer and all places filled for both girls and boys, the need for the Y7 house was reviewed. The College returned to 11-16 houses from September 2014. Peel served its purpose for about twenty years and the staff can be proud of the fact that their welcoming and nurturing provision turned a declining boarding roll into one growing to full capacity. The teaching of mathematics which had been squeezed into former science labs and temporaries was provided with a new Mathematics block in 2001, the year of the College celebrating its fiftieth anniversary.

~

In 2005, the College 1st Rugby XV had an unbeaten season for the first time in its history and two College players were picked for England honours at U16 level. In 2006, the College achieved the best GCSE results since the examination started and Dominic Findlay took over from Victoria Musgrave as Principal. Dominic left to become Head of Langley School in 2007. He was succeeded by Melvyn Roffe from Old Swinford Hospital. Melvyn became the Chairman of the Boarding Schools Association in 2009, one of only four Heads of State boarding schools who have chaired both SBSA and BSA. In that year, the College A level candidates achieved the best A level results ever, '*a remarkable 70% of which were at A or B grades*', not bad for a comprehensive state school.

11. Academies

In the same year, 2009, Wymondham College became an Academy with Norfolk County Council's strong support, the first State Boarding school to move to Academy status. The College would no longer be dependent on or controlled by the County Council in any way, with the last remaining links over curriculum and staff terms of service severed. Most such control had ended some time before but the College remained very much part of the Norfolk family of schools. Wymondham had strengthened that family by becoming the lead sponsor of the Thetford Academy, sharing its skills and expertise with other schools across the County.

By 2011, the Academy movement had already grown to over a thousand schools, spread across the country. The initial idea had been developed by Andrew Adonis (now Lord Adonis) when he served as Tony Blair's Education Advisor in the 1990s. Adonis has written of his frustration at the low level of performance of many of England's secondary schools, what he calls 'secondary modern comprehensives'. These were schools which had an all ability intake but which were failing most of their pupils through low aspirations, poor leadership and weak governance. In 1997, in half of all state secondary schools, only 30% of their Y11 pupils achieved five or more GCSE A-C grades – a damning indictment of what Alastair Campbell, Tony Blair's spokesman, called 'bog-standard comprehensives'.

Adonis identified the City Technology Colleges (CTCs) set up by Kenneth Baker and Sir Cyril Taylor under the Conservative government of the 1980s and 1990s as a model which could be developed under Labour into the 1990s. These CTCs developed under Tony Blair's Labour

Government with Adonis as Schools Minister into first City Academies and then just Academies. They had some of the same features, a specialist curriculum focus, independence of Local Authority control, a longer school day, business sponsorship and a system of governance that made them 'independent state schools'.

By 2015, there will be over 4,400 such schools, primary and secondary, all over England. That means that roughly 60% of all secondary schools and 13% of all primary schools will be Academies. Fifteen of these academies are State Boarding schools and the number is growing fast. When Andrew Adonis speaks to conferences about Academies, he looks back to his own schooling at Kingham Hill School in Oxfordshire. When his Cypriot father's wife left the family, Andrew and his sister were taken into the care of Camden Social Services. Andrew became one of the 'looked-after' children whose educational outcomes have been so poor. But thanks to the feisty manager of his Camden Council Children's Home, he was given a boarding place at Kingham Hill, paid for by Camden. Adonis has described Kingham Hill:

'…..*a boarding school in Oxfordshire with a foundation dedicated to the welfare of disadvantaged boys – and more recently girls. I owe more than I can possibly say, or ever repay, to Kingham Hill and to those who supported me while I was there. It transformed my life…*'

~

In September 2011, Harefield Academy in Hillingdon became the first Academy to open a new boarding house, providing fifty boarding places for boys and girls from 11 to 18. The Academy, which is a specialist Sports College, attracted talented basketball players and gymnasts amongst the first boarding intake. It has a special relationship with

Watford Football Club which includes the Club sponsoring boarding places for talented young footballers. The Academy has named the new boarding house 'Lord Adonis House' and was delighted that he accepted their invitation to formally open the building in 2012.

With a budget of £3.9 million, Adonis House was planned and agreed under the Labour Government of Gordon Brown and the project could have been cancelled when Michael Gove became Secretary of State for Education in the Coalition Government of 2010. However, the Academy programme started under Labour has continued under David Cameron and has accelerated over the past five years. Funding for Lord Adonis House was not finally agreed until 2010. Andrew Adonis, former Labour Education Minister, opened the new house built with funding approved by Conservative Minister, Michael Gove – a very unusual example of the two parties agreeing policy. Over the same period of five years, two more Academies have opened new boarding houses. In 2012, the Priory LSST opened the Robert de Cheney House on their Lincoln campus, with provision for up to sixty 6th form boarders, boys and girls, with a focus on boarding places for students from Ministry of Defence families serving at nearby RAF Wadington.

At Tidworth in Wiltshire, in the middle of the Salisbury Plain, Casteldown School was a comprehensive with poor examination results and patterns of behaviour. It had been placed in Special Measures by Ofsted but under a new Head was making progress when the DfE suggested to the Governors of the independent Wellington College they might like to partner the school as an Academy. Wellington was founded by Queen Victoria and the Prime Minister in 1859 as a memorial to the Duke of Wellington and located in palatial buildings in Berkshire. The idea that the school should sponsor a failing comprehensive over fifty miles away did not seem at first to be sensible.

But the two schools had some things in common. The first boys to attend Wellington College were the orphans of Army Officers and the sons of serving Officers. Over 40% of the pupils at Castledown were from Army families stationed in Tidworth Garrison. Two former Wellington students put up the £2 million sponsorship which the new Academy needed. By 2008, a new Principal had been appointed and the Wellington Academy opened in 2009 in the existing buildings, with a new school to be built by 2010 as a State Boarding School.

Anthony Seldon, now Sir Anthony, who retired as the Master of Wellington in 2015, has been a prime mover of the project from the start. It is his conviction that 'the DNA of Wellington', a commitment to 'all-round education' based on eight aptitudes, can be transferred to the new Academy with profit to both schools. The new school would have a strong house system, a commitment to outdoor activities, a Combined Cadet Force and provision for boarders. Wellington has over 700 boarders amongst the 850 students at the College. In the planning for the new Academy buildings, provision for 100 boarders, 50 girls and 50 boys, in two houses was included from the start. In addition to the £2 million of private sponsorship, the Government has invested £30 million to build the school.

Wellington Academy's new buildings were opened in 2011 by HRH Duke of York and it now has over 1000 students and a Sixth Form. The school specialises in languages and in business and enterprise, and has a range of community facilities, a sports and fitness centre, a bowling green, an indoor shooting range and a beauty treatment centre. The school's media centre provides Casteldown Radio, a local station. Within two years of its opening the new Academy was recognised by Ofsted and in the local league tables as one of the best performing schools in Wiltshire, said to have made outstanding progress.

Seldon has encouraged the Heads and Governors of many HMC schools to become involved in sponsoring Academies. Dulwich, Eton, Westminster and the King Edward VI Foundation Schools in Birmingham have all sponsored academies. A further sixteen HMC schools have co-sponsored academies and six have sponsored new Free Schools, including the four sponsors of the London Academy of Excellence.

New Academy building projects have attracted world class architects, including Zaha Hadid, Foster Partners and Nicholas Hare. Some of their exotic buildings have also been criticised for being too costly and not fit for purpose. When he was Education Secretary, Michael Gove, told a conference for Academy Heads that his Department would not be *getting Richard Rogers to design your school; we won't be getting any award-winning architects to design it, because no one in this room is here to make architects richer.*

Nevertheless, many have celebrated the commissioning of these projects as demonstrating that schools should have exciting buildings, provided that they are fit to teach, learn and live in. Victorian England is remembered for some harsh aspects of schooling but it was also a time when great Victorian architects were commissioned to build magnificent schools, for London's St Paul's School and for the City of London School, for Wellington College in Berkshire and for Clifton College in Bristol.

153

Eton College's involvement in the Academies programme is particularly interesting as Eton was one of the few major public schools which chose not to develop overseas campuses as clones of themselves. The first such campus to be established was Harrow's Bangkok development in 1998. By 2014, there were 39 overseas campuses established by British schools educating over 22,500 students, eleven are in the Middle East and ten in Mainland China. Dulwich has set up a network of seven such campuses in Asia. Wellington has built two campuses in China which even mimic the architecture of Wellington College's Berkshire buildings.

Eton has no such overseas clones but has become the sponsor of an academy in the village of Holyport, just outside Windsor across the Thames from Eton. Using the site of a former Local Authority special school, Holyport College is a Free School, an Academy approved in July 2012 which had no previous existence as a school. With a Government investment of £15 million in buildings and a planned capacity of 500 11-18 boys and girls, the school is non-selective and roughly half boarding. The first Principal is Walter Boyle, former Vice Principal of Wymondham College and some of the curriculum and boarding arrangements at Holyport follow the Wymondham model. When full, Holyport will be a school with about 50% full boarding places with day pupils encouraged to share the same opportunities as boarders and to take part in an extended school day.

Rather than making a significant financial contribution, Eton College has provided expertise. The Governors of the new school include the current Head, Lower Master, Director of Curriculum, a Housemaster and a Master of

Eton College, and the Clerk is the Eton Clerk and Legal Advisor. Holyport pupils have access to some of Eton's wonderful sports facilities, including rowing on the Eton Dorney Olympic course. Old Etonians have paid £140,000 for Holyport's Astroturf pitch and the College has loaned a Latin and Art teacher to Holyport, free of charge. Holyport received its first pupils into Y7 and Y9 in 2014/5 and will open a 6th Form when these Y9s reach Y12 in 2017/8. The College was formally opened by Her Majesty the Queen in November 2014, with 122 pupils on site including 55 boarders.

~

State Boarding schools have benefitted since 2013 from the very considerable influence of a second 'boarding Lord'. John Nash was a barrister and was involved in business and finance before following his political interests onto the Board of the Centre for Policy Studies. A strong supporter of the Conservative Party, John became Schools Minister under the Coalition government in 2013 on being created Lord Nash of Ewelme. He is also co-founder of the charity Future which has sponsored academies and he is a strong supporter of State Boarding schools.

Speaking at the SBSA conference in 2014, Lord Nash reminded his audience of Heads and Governors that his own personal experience of growing up in South London led him to appreciate the benefits of a boarding opportunity. He had no thoughts of boarding until his mother died and he was sent away to Milton Abbey School in Dorset,

'...where I was certainly the only child who had not previously boarded and one of the very few not to have failed to get into Eton. I was regarded as a right pleb – but I fairly quickly learnt to appreciate the experience and I know how much good it did me and how much *trouble I would have probably got into had I gone to school at home. So my personal experience leads me to be highly supportive of the boarding experience and all the evidence is that it can be very transformative for the right children....'*

From this perspective, Lord Nash has supported a number of projects which have increased the availability of boarding places in state schools and in making these available to pupils from poorer backgrounds. One of these is the development of Durand Academy in South London. The Head, Greg Martin, took over the school in 1986 and grasped every opportunity to break free from Lambeth Education Authority, becoming Grant Maintained and then a Foundation School, before encouraging his Governors to apply for Academy status. The school is a four-form entry Primary, the largest in Lambeth, serving an area with about 97% African Caribbean families. It has developed a reputation for very high standards, both of pupil progress and of discipline. Greg Martin was knighted in 2013 for 'services to education'.

Durand shares its two sites with two social enterprises which are operated by a limited company, London Horizons Ltd. Horizons Accommodation offers fifty rooms in London in a mix of singles and doubles. Horizons Health Club has a swimming pool, gym, sauna, steam room and organised yoga and Pilates classes. Both enterprises are very profitable and the Company has used these profits to improve the school's facilities, including access to the swimming pool and an astro-turf pitch.

But Durand Academy has also attracted controversy. In 2014, the Audit Commission published its investigation into the Education Funding Agency's oversight of the Durand Academy Trust. They were looking into the links between Durand Academy's Trust and the London Horizons Company's commercial operations. Were these links sufficiently transparent?

Sir Greg Martin was called before the Commons Public Accounts Committee and faced hostile questioning. Members expressed surprise at the size of his salary as Head, £230,000 in 2012/3, and his additional personal earnings of £160,000 as sole director of the Leisure Centre. The final straw for MPs was the news that he ran a 'dating website' from the school address. Sir Greg insisted that there was nothing wrong with any of these arrangements and that income from the Leisure Centre subsidised school lunches, evening child care and is now being used to subsidise boarding places.

Durand Academy now educates over a thousand pupils, with an Early Years Unit, a Junior School, a Middle School for Y7 and Y8 and a secondary school for 13-18 students. This will have boarding provision and will be based in West Sussex. The Academy Trust bought the premises of the former St Cuthman's School in Steadham near Midhurst and applied for planning permission in 2013 to convert the site into a boarding school for 375 pupils. Planning was refused.

The DfE has pledged £17.3 million to support this novel development with the Durand Trust providing a further £5 million. The Academy Trust has meanwhile started to bus groups of forty eight Y9 pupils each week from Stockwell to Steadham. They spend Mondays at school in Stockwell, then travel to Steadham for a shortened school week, Tuesday to Thursday, with three nights boarding in the existing school buildings, returning on Fridays to Stockwell.

The plan to develop a boarding school for South London children inside the South Downs National Park has generated strong and vocal local opposition. Objection from another source has come from the leaders of the State Boarding world. Roy Page, the Head of the Royal Grammar School, High Wycombe, chose as the theme of his Chairman's address to the 2013 SBSA conference the problem which many SBSA schools face in finding the capital to maintain and improve their boarding buildings. While thanking Lord Nash as Minister responsible for schools and the Academies programme for his very welcome support to SBSA through funding for staff training, Roy Page went on to say:

'....... *for two years now we have been seeking clarity and security from the Government concerning capital investment in the fabric of State Boarding schools. We are in dire need of it. Lord Nash spoke to us in June, and indeed came to this very school in July, and was eloquent in his praise for State Boarding schools. But we have not been given the means to secure their future. Meanwhile, £17m has been given – no questions asked - to a new academy in Sussex, to an organisation and a Headmaster with no experience in boarding, a funding decision that – quite rightly in my view - is being queried by the Public Accounts Committee and the National Audit Office.'*

In Durand's plans for their boarding school in Sussex, they announced that there would be no boarding fees charged to parents. Income from 'pupil premium' payments, the enhanced Government funding linked to pupils who receive free school meals, together with income donated to the Trust by the commercial operations of the Leisure Centre and Accommodation businesses would cover the costs of the boarding places.

Durand Academy has published a defence of its plans and has pointed out that they are based on the assumption that all staffing costs from 8.15 am to 9.30 pm would be covered by the school budget. 'Boarding' would only be charged for the costs of overnight staffing supervision for four nights per week in term-time. There would be no weekend provision. They explained that they did seek the expert advice of colleagues from Wellington College in verifying their proposals. Their very low figures, most recently estimated at £2300 per year per boarder, provoked a strong challenge from SBSA, all of whose schools charge around £10,000 per year per boarder.

Melvyn Roffe, when Principal of Wymondham College, wrote to the Minister to point out that this cost was 'implausibly low'.

'It lacks clarity about staff accommodation and salaries and fails to take into account the impact of spreading the school's budget thinly across such an extended day. If we were allowed to do the same at Wymondham College, we would soon see a significant impact on our positive outcomes for students due to larger class sizes, constrained curriculum choice and reduced support available,' he wrote.

Nevertheless, the Durand proposals for a *'cut-price Eton in the countryside for city kids'* have received strong support from across the political spectrum. Kate Hoey, their local Labour MP for Vauxhall, Michael Gove MP, former Conservative Secretary of State for Education, Vernon Coker MP, former Labour Schools Minister, the Rt Hon David Laws, former Liberal Democrat Schools Minister, and Mark Dunn, Former Conservative Chair of West Sussex Council, have all written in support of the Durand Academy proposals. How many other state schools can claim support from such a glittering political array! For the moment, the school will continue to bus groups of Y9 pupils from Stockwell to Sussex for part of their school week and initial reports suggest that they are very much enjoying the experience.

Meanwhile, not far away in another corner of West Sussex, in West Horsham, disadvantaged boys and girls from London and other urban areas have been enjoying an excellent boarding school experience. In many cases, this is provided at no cost to their parents, or in many cases, their single parent. It could be argued that Greg Martin's Durand pupils are simply following in the footsteps of the thousands of boys and girls, who have been wearing the bluecoat uniform of Christ's Hospital for centuries. They are both enjoying the profits of successful business, whether that is a Stockwell leisure club or the City of London. The Durand pupils wear a distinctive uniform just as their 'Housey' contemporaries do – it's just more modern!

12. Specialist Schools

One of the Wymondham Governors, impressed by our ability to extract capital and revenue funds from Central Government, quipped:

'If they ever show interest in developing a national centre for kiSwahili and Tap-dancing and invite bids, you two would put in a convincing bid for Wymondham to have just that ambition.'

Needless to say, the Government never did invite bids for a national centre for these exotic 'specialisms' but the State Boarding schools as a group were very active in developing specialisms beyond their own particular expertise in providing boarding places for those who want and those who need them. From 1994, several followed the Government's Specialist Schools initiative.

This started with thirty five schools being designated *'Technology Colleges'*. They had to raise £100,000 of private sponsorship which the Government matched and then enhanced their revenue budgets. In succeeding years, Languages, Sport, the Arts, Business and Enterprise, Engineering, Maths and Computing, Science, Humanities and Music were all added to the list. Many schools have been able to follow two or more areas of Specialism.

The Initiative was endorsed by the Labour Government of 1997. In the White Paper of 2001, it was seen as a means of driving up standards across all secondary schools. Initially, the target was for 50% of all secondary schools becoming 'specialist'. By 2008, about 88% of maintained secondary schools had become 'specialist'. With the arrival of the Coalition Government of 2010, Michael Gove decided that the resources committed to the Specialist Schools Initiative, by then £450 million per year, should be distributed to all secondary schools through the Dedicated Schools Grant. The Specialist Schools Initiative was wound up from April 2011.

Eleven of the State Boarding schools still refer to their 'Specialist School' commitment and many others will have had some 'specialism' before the Initiative ended. St George's Academy, Harpenden, lists five: Technology, Information Technology, Maths, Science, and Languages. Skegness Grammar School has three: Maths and Computing, Sport and Science. Adam's Grammar School has Technology and Languages, as does Ashby School. Wellington Academy has Languages and Business and Enterprise, Sir Roger Manwood's School has Languages and Maths and Computing. The other five schools, Burford School (Technology), Haydon Bridge High School (Sports), QE Academy, Crediton (Technology), De Aston School (Maths and Computing) and Dallam School (Languages) each refer to one.

Many SBSA schools saw this initiate as a means of accessing badly need capital development and revenue funding. Because of their need to finance and fill boarding places, they have become much more entrepreneurial than most state secondary schools and could apply skills and lessons from this area of their activity to curriculum initiatives.

~

There was a time when several SBSA schools had a 'specialist' interest in farming or horticulture. Burford School in the Cotswolds even had its own school farm. That farm has sadly now been lost but Burford School still has a large and very successful boarding house for boys and girls in a school which has recently been recognised by the Schools Minister as one of the best ninety secondary schools in the Country.

Brymore Academy, formerly Brymore School, was founded as a State Boarding Technical School of Agriculture. When the 1944 Act was implemented, Somerset, like Norfolk, had grammar schools in the market towns and many of its elementary schools became secondary modern schools. But, also like Norfolk, Somerset was a very rural county with no Technical provision. The County established Brymore to serve the whole of Somerset, based on the Brymore estate near Bridgwater. Today, the school is a boys' 11-17 boarding Academy at the foot of the Quantock Hills.

Brymore has always been a relatively small all-boys school, with 150 boarders in a total roll of 200. There are 'four cornerstones' for life at Brymore, the 110 acre school farm, the 1 acre walled gardens, the fully equipped workshops and their strong commitment to competitive sports. Each of these plays a major role in every boy's time at the school. The school day starts with farm duties at 6.30 am and ends after afternoon school with more such duties. All the farm 'departments', dairy herd, beef animals, pig herd, poultry and the flock of sheep are run by the boys themselves with senior boys acting as 'Heads of Department' under the overall control of the professional farm manager.

The farming operation, along with the gardens, reinforces the school's aim of instilling responsibility in the boys to prepare them for the world of work, both within the farming community and beyond. Classes in all the academic subjects are small and the school prides itself on stretching and motivating every boy to achieve his best; all are encouraged to 'go beyond their limits'.

As a result, although the school caters for all abilities, 23% of students achieved A/A* in GCSE English last year, placing the school in the top 1% of the country for progress. Brymore is regularly in the top 2% of schools in the country for student progress across all subjects. 88% of students achieved 5A*-Cs in 2014 way above the National %. Many of them would not have achieved such results elsewhere. Brymore teaches boys to value hard work and commitment – hence, the motto 'Diligentia et Labore'.

Sport has always been important to the school, with many voluntary team sports in addition to the timetabled PE and games periods. A key tradition is the school run – "Chads Hill" –which is three and a quarter miles. All boys are expected to run it once a week. Brymore has a long history of boys who have gone on to represent Somerset at rugby and athletics with many going to achieve national recognition. The school takes great pride in offering 'experience to last a lifetime' and boarding at Brymore received a major boost in 2005/7 with the allocation of a Government capital grant of £3.4 million to build a new boarding house and re-furbish the existing houses.

~

A school which has always had very close links with the Military is the Duke of York's Royal Military Academy (DYRMA). Founded by Royal Warrant, this school opened at Chelsea in 1803 as an orphanage for the children of soldiers who fell in battle. It was Britain's first co-educational school funded and administered by the state through the Ministry of Defence. In 1903, the school moved to its present site in Kent and in 2010, the school became a member of SBSA becoming an Academy sponsored by the

Ministry of Defence, moving from the independent to the state sector.

The school admits boys and girls at 11 with many coming from military families although there are an increasing number of pupils whose families do not have that background. When the school became an Academy, it received £24m to fund a building programme and now has superb facilities on its 150 acre site in Kent. The school's military ethos and heritage is still very much part of what it offers, together with the traditional values of self-discipline, self-reliance, spirituality, leadership and respect for others.

All pupils at the DYRMA, known as 'Yorkies', are boarders, currently 470 boys and girls including 105 6th Formers. Parents just pay a boarding fee, as education is free, and this is currently £10,995, very much in line with other SBSA schools. As most parents are still serving with the Armed Forces and can claim the Continuity of Education Allowance (CEA) which more than covers the cost, most only pay the 10% parental contribution, currently £1,099.50 per year, which for military families is a bargain.

DYRMA celebrates its military tradition with Ceremonial Parades, supported by the ninety strong marching band, and the full Trooping of the Colour Ceremony at the centre of the school's Grand Day. All pupils wear the cap badge of the unit in which their parent is serving on their Dress Blue uniforms for the day. The school's own Regimental Sergeant Major ensures that standards of drill are kept impeccably high!

~

Language learning is a very much more universal in schools than an interest in either agriculture or the military and several SBSA schools achieved Language College status before the Specialist Schools Initiative was wound up. Four of them, Adams Grammar School in Shropshire, Ashby School in Leicestershire, Dallam School in Cumbria and Hockerill Anglo-European College in Hertfordshire, all developed a Language Specialism but with a range of intensity.

When William Adams founded a grammar school in 1656, in his home area of Newport, Shropshire, he was already established as a successful member of the Haberdashers' Company in London and so entrusted his school to them. The Haberdashers have an on–going involvement in England's schools, including independent, state primary and secondary, CTCs and most recently Academies. Adams Grammar School today is Newport's very successful boys' 11-18 grammar school. Girls join the boys in the 6th Form. The school has recently been given an 'outstanding' judgment by Ofsted and also has 'outstanding' boarding provision for about one hundred boarders. Junior boarders in years 7-9 occupy Longford Hall, a 'beautiful Georgian mansion set in one hundred acres of grounds with magnificent views of the surrounding countryside'. At 14/15, boarders move to the main school site.

Under the current Head, the school has maintained its reputation for academic excellence but also aims to develop confident, articulate young men and women, who are interesting, balanced and independent people who care for each other.

~

In contrast to this grammar school, both Ashby School and Dallam School are large mixed comprehensives. Ashby with 1600 14-19 students including 500 6th Formers is a Leicestershire Upper School, now an Academy, judged by

Ofsted this year to be 'a good school' with 'outstanding' boarding. It was one of the first schools to get Language College status and has held the British Council International School Award since 2011. This award is giving to schools which have a global dimension to lessons across the curriculum, in Ashby's case including international poetry in English, international conflict in Art, World music in Music lessons and international trade in Business Studies.

There is a very long tradition of boys' boarding going back four hundred years to the days of Ashby Grammar School. The Georgian boarding house, School House, is at the heart of the town, next to the Parish Church and the remains of Ashby Castle. When the Governors built a new house for their Headmaster there was space in the upper floors for boys to board. Their parents paid him a capitation fee for the privilege. This was another classic example of the Head of a market town grammar schools enhancing his meagre income from the Governors, just as Heads had in Louth and in Ripon. In the Victorian period, School House was expanded with a wing of dormitories built over a dining hall, to give the House a capacity of about 40 boys. Many similar schools eventually became independent schools but Ashby Grammar School remained the grammar school for the boys of the town right up to comprehensive reorganisation in 1972. Then the boys' and the girls' grammar schools combined to become a 14-18 comprehensive Upper School.

Through the 1990s the boarding numbers at Ashby were falling as they were in many State boarding houses. John Williams, the Director of Boarding, was at that inaugural meeting in 1990 which led to the formation of STABIS and then SBSA and well remembers the lack of interest showed by his Local Authority in the future of his Boarding House. By the late 1990s, they were down to just 30 boys, when John's background in Language Schools provided him with a collection of invaluable contacts who knew where potential boarders could be recruited. As it became clear that there were families in Europe, in Hong Kong and in fact all over the world who had British or EU passports and could access UK State Schools, boarding numbers began to creep up.

The current Director of Boarding, Xenia Elias, has an interesting background. A graduate in psychology with a business rather than a teaching background, she can devote all her time and energies to the community of boarders she leads. Like some of the first Eton College Heads of House who were in fact Dames rather than Housemasters, she now runs the House, holds the budgets, organises and recruits the staff and offers the boarding places, all to boys. As numbers rose, from 30 to 45 by 2002, John and Xenia re-arranged the existing space to create more boarding capacity within the Georgian and Victorian shell of the building. They had a business plan for what was essentially a highly entrepreneurial unit operating within a state school.

Realising that the limited money they were allowed to carry forward year on year was never going to be enough to fund new accommodation, they bid for funds to the Department for Education. As other schools, like Wymondham College, were given large grants, Ashby received nothing. It must have been difficult for them and other struggling SBSA schools, not to share the sense of injustice which faced the man who had just one talent in Jesus' parable: 'for to everyone who has, more will be given, and he will have abundance; but from him who has not, even what he has will be taken away.' (Matthew 25 v29 RSV).

168

Many schools closed their boarding houses and SBSA shrank to just 32 schools.

Then, with support from BSA's Director, Hilary Moriarty, and thanks to Lord Adonis' strong commitment to State Boarding, Ashby's bid for capital to develop more boarding places was approved. In 2012, thanks to a total investment of almost £3 million, including £2.4 million from the DfE, the school was able to double the number of boarding places to 75, with a new wing offering 2-bed en-suite rooms for 6th Formers.

All meals for boarders are prepared by House staff and served in a spacious dining room to which boarders can invite their day-pupil friends. The whole emphasis is to make School House an attractive home, with good art on the walls, comfortable common rooms and access to the excellent facilities on the school site just over the boarding house garden hedge. While using these, boarders are supervised by the team of boarding House staff, which include a Nursing Sister and a living-in Director.

As Xenia said, *'we appoint staff who will commit themselves to looking after our boarders – that is their focus and they don't have to come here to do their marking in the evening or prepare their lessons; their job is boarding and we pay them well for it.'*

~

The third SBSA school with a Language Specialism, Dallam School, on the southern edge of the Lake District, must have one of the most attractive settings of all the SBSA schools. Now an Academy with 1000 11-18 boys and girls including 200 in the 6th Form, there are about 120 boarders living in the premises of the former Heversham Grammar School now improved and extended thanks to a capital investment of £1.8 million. The most recent Ofsted report on this boarding provision rated it as 'outstanding' in all categories. Boarders were said to be *'part of an exceptionally inclusive community and enjoy extremely positive and tolerant relationships with staff and each other. (They) refer to the very diverse and culturally rich nature of the boarding environment, which supports them to develop friendships and gain in confidence...Boarders benefit from a school that fully embraces equal opportunities. Disability is not seen as a barrier to achievement or equality....'*

6th form students at Dallam are offered a full range of A levels and the school also offers the International Baccalaureate and the IB Career Related Programme. With a vision of *'learning for all, learning for life'*, it is a centre for community learning, leisure and the arts as well as a licensed outdoor education centre and the UK's first Adventure Learning School. The Adventure Learning ethos influences all school activities as Dallam makes full use of its setting at the gateway to the Lake District.

~

The SBSA school which has taken the specialism of Languages to the most successful level is Hockerill Anglo-European College in Bishop's Stortford, yet the school started very modestly. In 1980, Essex combined two Secondary Modern Boarding Schools, Fyfield School and Kennylands School to form a new mixed Essex Secondary Modern Boarding School using the premises of the former Teacher Training College at Hockerill, Bishop's Stortford. Richard Perry became the first Head with about three hundred boarders living in the old premises. Alison Atkins, with whom I had worked in Louth as she was the former Head of Cordeaux High School, took over in 1986 and the school continued as one of the very few former Secondary Modern boarding schools maintained by a local Authority.

Under the next Head, the school Governors' decided to seek Grant Maintained status and to leave the control of Essex County Council. When Dr Rob Guthrie became Head of the School in 1996, it had a falling boarding roll, no 6th Form and no 'unique selling point' – it was just one of the dwindling number of State Boarding schools with little academic distinction and a very uncertain future.

By the time he retired in 2008, the school had become Hockerill Anglo-European College and one of the most successful comprehensive schools in England. In November 2011, Hockerill became the first state school to be awarded the accolade of the Sunday Times International Baccalaureate School of the Year award.

The first stage of this development was to establish a 6th Form. When applications to do so failed for two successive years, the school made arrangements with the local Catholic Secondary School with a 6th Form to 'host' Hockerill 16-19 students to enable them to continue as boarders. Having demonstrated the success of this informal arrangement, the school's third attempt to form a 6th Form was approved and the school became the Hockerill Anglo-European College from 1998.

Before Rob Guthrie took over Hockerill School, he had been the Head of the Rome International School, having previously been a Housemaster at Stonyhurst, the Boys' Independent Boarding School founded by the Jesuits. He came to Hockerill with links to Catholic schools, experience of boarding and of leading a school which offered the IB. The Catholic link provided the means of starting a 6th Form, boarding had always been part of the Hockerill School culture and the IB was a natural choice for taking the school forward into a much more promising future.

171

A very gifted linguist and teacher, Mike Ullman, became Head of Modern Languages at Hockerill and suggested a radical innovation, teaching subjects like History and Geography not in English but in French or in German. This took the concept of Specialist Language College to a whole new level and provided a wonderful basis for further progress in Languages into the 6th Form, where the IB became Hockerill's post-16 curriculum. Under the point score system which the DfE devised for comparing A level results with IB results, many of those whose schools stuck to AS and A levels found that the advantage was strongly in favour of the IB schools. Their average point score at 18+ gave the IB schools what others saw as an unfair advantage. Hockerill Anglo-European not only benefitted from this advantage but exploited it to the full, becoming, according to the Independent newspaper, the *'Country's top-performing State School for post 16* results' for six successive years, from 2006 to 2012.

When Ofsted visited in 2007, the College was judged 'outstanding' in all judgements, a ringing endorsement of the changes which Rob Guthrie had initiated nine years before. In the follow-up Inspection in 2011, this outstanding judgement was confirmed and in the 2012 Ofsted Boarding Inspection, the College was again judged to be outstanding in all boarding judgements.

Mike Ullman's work had been acknowledged at National level when he was awarded the Guardian Teacher of the Year Award in 2005 for his work at Hockerill and his organisation of the College's extensive Exchange programme. Sadly, he died in 2010 but the College remembers his contribution with a plaque in his memory in the Mike Ullmann Building.

Since 1998, the College has doubled in size, with over 700 students around a third of whom are boarders from Europe and beyond. The provision of a two year IB course from 16 is particularly attractive to students from Germany. They can come with their EU passports and complete their IB course in two years gaining access to the best three year degree courses in the UK. The College's proximity to Stansted Airport means that it is very accessible to all European capitals and also has excellent rail links with London. The College has also proved attractive to many parents whose children have attended International Schools abroad. They have found that boarding at Hockerill allows them to re-enter the UK system while their parents continue to work in Europe.

The Hockerill staff are unusually cosmopolitan, with a high proportional of bilingual teachers. The College has strong links with Nottingham University for the training of Language Teachers and has developed a network of partner schools throughout Europe with cultural and exchange opportunities for students.

In 2006, the College gained a further specialist status, becoming a Music College in recognition of the excellence of its music provision. There is a recording studio, a music technology suite and over three hundred students receive individual tuition weekly, contribute to the College Orchestra and Choir and have many opportunities for performance in the UK and abroad.

Hockerill has come a long way from its modest origins to the highly successful Academy which is regularly featured in Ministerial speeches today.

13. 6th Form Boarding

Wymondham College's new 6th Form Boarding House

We became boarding parents when our younger son decided to stay in Louth. He could have moved with us to Norfolk either to go into the 6th form at Norwich School or to become the 'New Principal's' son in the Wymondham 6th Form. He was not keen to do either and asked about staying in Louth with his friends as a boarder in the small boys' boarding house which formed part of his school, King Edward VI School, Louth. So without ever intending to have a son at boarding school, we became boarding parents.

In England, parents become 'boarding parents' when their children go to Prep School at the age of seven – that must be tough for them and for their children. More become 'boarding parents' when their children go to secondary school at eleven. That is still young but easier for children to cope with the separation from the family, particularly if the school offers weekly boarding.

For many boys in the independent sector, transfer to senior school or to 'Public School' as many of them still style themselves, is at thirteen, just at the point when many boys are starting to go through all the turmoil that puberty involves. In some areas, state secondary schools also start at thirteen, for most of the comprehensive High Schools in Northumberland for example and for the selective Cranbrook School, a very successful mixed grammar school in Kent which is proud to be the only 13-18 state grammar school in the country.

In England up to 2013, pupils could leave school at sixteen, rising to seventeen in 2014 and to eighteen from 2015. This has produced a culture in the UK where post-16 education, or 'the Sixth Form', has been seen in the past as the privilege of the more academic minority. My American High School Principal friends could not get over the fact that, through the 1980s and 1990s, a high proportion of UK sixteen-year olds were allowed to leave full-time education. In their system, such pupils would be thought of as 'drop-outs' prone to a high level of youth crime and general social disapproval!

From 2015/6, all young people will be required to stay in full time education until they are eighteen. Yet old structures remain. We still talk about 'the Sixth Form' as if the two years of education for 16-18 year olds were somehow very different from the previous five years from eleven. 'Sixth Forms' still have a ring of the academic élite. The proper terms, Year 12 and Year 13, are just not used in the way Y10 and Y11 are now used. Who now in state schools talks about the 4th and 5th Years? We have a chain of 'Sixth Form Colleges' across the country which includes some of the most successful routes into the élite University world of Oxford and Cambridge.

SBSA developments reflect this in the growing popularity of 6th Form boarding. A good example is the small family style boarding house for 6th Form boys at Colchester Royal Grammar School in Essex. The school has a history of scholarship dating back to the sixteenth century, and is today one of the most successful selective grammar schools, the top state school for A level results according to the government performance tables, with an outstanding record for university entrance. In 2014 CRGS students received 40 Oxbridge offers and over 20 offers from Medical Schools. It became an academy in 2012 and was designated a National Teaching School and a National Support School in 2013.

There is now a strong market nationally for boarding at sixteen. At that age, young people can benefit hugely from time away from their family home, time to become more independent, more able to prepare for the separation which will come for most at eighteen and time to establish new habits of study and to explore new relationships. Our 6th Form boarder son came back to us for most weekends and although he probably missed his home comforts, we certainly missed him much more. In our case, it enabled him to stay with his friends and thanks to a benevolent and strong House team, we knew he was safe.

~

Another specialist boarding state school is Welbeck Defence College, the national Sixth Form College for 'students who see their future career as engineers within the Military and Defence community'. About 90% of the 185 students who join each year for the first year of their A level

176

studies in Mathematics and Science are funded by the Ministry of Defence. They have applied via their sponsoring service, the Royal Navy, the Army, the Royal Air Force or the Civil Service Defence Engineering and Science Group. 10% of entrants are privately funded and do not have the same commitment to a career in the military or civil service.

Welbeck was set up originally as a male only Sixth Form college specific to the Army with a serving Army Officer as Principal. It is now independent within the state sector with its own Board of Governors and led by a civilian Principal. It admits both men and women, for careers in all three Armed Services and has lost its close ties to the UK Ministry of Defence. After Welbeck, successful students go on to a degree at University, supported by a Bursary scheme and with a requirement to take part in the activities of a University Support Unit. After their degree, they then go on to Officer Training with the Armed Services or Initial Professional Training.

~

In Winchester, Peter Symonds 6th Form College has been an open access college since 1974. It now caters for up to 2,900 students a year from all over central Hampshire and claims to have a catchment area of 8,000 miles, as it provides 16-19 places for students from the Falkland Islands. Most of the boarders do not have to travel so far! Based on Winchester's former boys' grammar school, it is now one of the leading 6th Form Colleges in England where students achieve excellent A level results, year after year. At the most recent Ofsted assessment, every area of the college was graded as outstanding. At the end of their visit the inspectors commented that they had never participated in an Inspection with such outstanding findings.

There are two boarding houses at Peter Symonds College: Falkland Lodge and School House. Both are co-educational and both are on the campus itself. Falkland Lodge was opened in September 1998 and provides accommodation in single or twin-bedded rooms while School House is a handsome Victorian building in which students share 2, 3 or 4 bedded rooms. Peter Symonds Sixth Form College sends more students to Oxbridge each year than hundreds of other state schools combined and is seen by many as Oxford's main state feeder school

As they operate under different regulations to those which apply to State Secondary schools, some Sixth Form Colleges have been able to offer places to overseas students even though they may not have UK or EU passports. Peter Symonds is considering doing this from 2017. Richard Huish 6th Form College in Taunton, another Ofsted 'outstanding' college, is already offering such places and is building a new boarding house to expand boarding provision to 120 places. They have to charge the full cost of both education and boarding for these places and currently receive £12,000 per year for overseas pupils from parents compared with a budget allocation of £4,560 per UK pupil from the DfE. This makes them competitive on price with the independent sector schools who have of course been offering such places for many years. Peter Symonds estimates that the combined fee would be about £15,000 a year for a boarding place.

~

One of the areas where the independent sector has been dominant is sport at the highest level. A very interesting development at Beechen Cliff School in Bath is the link they have developed with Bath Rugby Club. The school already has a very strong reputation for excellent A level results and the new Sixth Form building completed in 2013 includes an upper floor which offers study bedrooms for 6th Formers and younger boys to board. Bath Rugby Club runs an Academy for promising young players from the Bath region and has formed a partnership with Beechen Cliff to provide a state school pathway to higher level Rugby.

Given the growing interest in 6th Form State boarding, it is not surprising that other 6th Form Colleges and SBSA schools are planning to expand their boarding provision. Boarding ceased at King Edward VI Grammar School, Louth in the 1990s, but the school now has a plan to open a 6th Form house adjacent to the school site in a building that was once a County Council residential unit. It will no doubt make a very attractive boarding house for 16-19 students from all over the UK and from families working all over the world who have UK or EU passports. The school had planned to open the new house for about 45 boarders in 2015 and had been assured that there was no planning difficulty. However, the building regulations experts have said that the House must now meet standards of sound insulation between rooms and floors that are demanded of hotels. Although hotel guests clearly have no wish to hear what is going on in the next room, those who have run school boarding houses have pointed out that it is safer for the staff to know what's going on in the dormitories!

14. Overseas Boarders

Over the last twenty years, many UK independent boarding schools have recruited pupils increasingly from overseas families. The total number of boarders in UK independent schools declined from about 110,000 in 1987 to about 65,000 in 2000, but then showed remarkable resilience by remaining at that level, give or take 2,000 for the last fourteen years, and rising slightly to the 2015 figure of just over 70,00. However, over these years, the number of boarders recruited from non-UK passport holders has steadily increased to about 25,000 in 2014, or about 38% of the total number of boarders.

It is true that these figures demonstrate the remarkable resilience of the UK independent boarding sector in finding new markets at a time of economic recession. The schools have become much more international and many have presented this as a positive feature, describing it as offering a 'global perspective not generally found at state-funded schools'. Others would argue that the over-riding pressure to fill boarding places with fee-paying clients, from whatever source could supply them, has diluted their unique ethos. For some schools, the 'unique selling point' as English Public Schools, which overseas parents found so attractive in the first place, may have changed beyond recognition.

About 37% of all these overseas boarders still come from Hong Kong and Mainland China although this proportion is now declining significantly. More boarders are coming from Europe, about 35%, and large numbers from both Russia and Nigeria. The numbers of boarders in independent schools who come from Armed Forces families who can draw the CEA has now dropped to just over 5,000.

The independent sector has been very successful in replacing UK boarding recruits and RAF and Army family recruits with boarders from the Far East, Europe, Russia and Africa.

~

In the 1990s, a new opportunity opened up for Chinese members of the Hong Kong civil service. Access to British boarding schools for the rich in Hong Kong and mainland China was already well established. Hong Kong Chinese civil servants who worked alongside expatriates were well aware that their British colleagues claimed generous boarding allowances to enable their children to   attend UK independent boarding schools and to be provided with free flights to UK and back each term.

When the British started to plan their withdrawal from the Colony, both they and the Chinese government wanted the Chinese civil servants who held British Hong Kong passports to stay in the Colony. So those who were needed to keep Hong Kong running smoothly were given the same terms of service as the expatriates, including opportunities for their children. As well as the senior Civil Servants of Chinese heritage, those eligible for these benefits included relatively junior civil service employees, police officers, port officials and other key workers.

If they chose to send them to the handful of UK maintained schools which still offered boarding places, the whole package was effectively free. The schools could not charge for teaching and the boarding fees were well within their Civil Service allowances. As boarding in the UK maintained sector became better publicised, the first few applications from Hong Kong based Chinese families came through. Boarders from Hong Kong began to arrive in our schools. These boarders did not at first have full UK passports but they did have the right of residence in the UK and that gave them access to State Boarding schools. Eventually, the Thatcher government granted 70,000 British passports to members of the Hong Kong civil service and their dependents

To meet this new development, an enterprising band of UK State Boarding Heads made regular recruiting visits to Hong Kong for much of the 1990's, alongside their independent school colleagues. They were helped by a former British Army Officer whose Academic Asia Educational Agency had been helping independent school to recruit students. As the numbers of students grew, support arrangements, including the provision of parents' consultation evenings in Hong Kong, were set up.

That was how I found myself travelling to the Far East on school business. I stayed as cheaply as possible in a very adequate Church of Scotland hostel in Kowloon and spent two or three days meeting new applicants and their parents. I carried out the interviews, tested the children's command of English and marked the tests. It was essential for all boarders to have sufficient English to access our courses.

In the evenings, I ran consultations for parents on their children's school reports. Towards the end of each visit, all the grateful mothers and fathers clubbed together to entertained me with a delicious banquet at the same Church of Scotland hostel. For the families, their children got a head start in the UK with access to UK Universities and careers. For the school, we filled boarding places with hard-working and disciplined students whose A level results helped us to climb the League Tables. From both points of view, the arrangement worked well.

When the British finally withdrew in 1997, we all thought that these arrangements would come to an end, but we underestimated the pragmatism of the Chinese. The government of Mainland China wanted to minimise change in Hong Kong so they actually maintained the provision of grants for the Civil Service. This led to the bizarre situation of some boarders at UK state schools having their boarding fees paid by the People's Republic of China, an arrangement which still operated ten years after the handover. The inevitable moment came when the number of boarders from Hong Kong, paid for by their Government as part of mainland China actually overtook the number of boarders from Norfolk, paid for by the County Council who had founded the College.

Not everyone was equally happy with the development which brought Hong Kong boarders to our College. As the numbers grew from one or two in each year-group, to a total of twenty or thirty across the school, we allocated places across all the Houses so that each pupil had at most four of five fellow Chinese in their house and so had to spend most of their day practising their English, just as their parents had hoped they would. But this was hard for them, particularly the youngest boarders. After a time, they took to gathering in the evenings in one of the Common Rooms or, in the summer time, under a particular tree, to meet up with their friends and talk Cantonese.

Other students began to resent these private conversations, feeling excluded from a language none of them knew or wanted to know. Staff began to overhear grumbling and comments about *'all these Chinese coming into the school'*. Attitudes could have easily hardened into open racism. Some over-imaginative staff were even afraid that these exclusive gatherings would lead to the Triad Gangs which were active in Hong Kong and in parts of London. But the Chinese showed little animosity to the other boarders and those who felt most resentful of private conversations were reminded that the students from Norwich or East Dereham also tended to meet to talk to each other of an evening. Because they did not all look alike, nobody bothered to comment. Nevertheless, a few cases of students actually quarrelling with each other had to be dealt with.

Once, we had a real fight between a small Chinese boy called David and one of the boys sharing his dormitory. David and his friend, Brian, arrived in Y7 in the same term and as they knew each other from home, their request to be put in the same House was accepted. But they were put in different dormitories to encourage them to make new friends. Although the staff claimed not to be able to tell them apart, they were actually very different characters.

Brian was outgoing, sociable and made friends easily with the other boys. David was much quieter, slightly devious and had very few friends. He decided to make himself more popular by teaching the boys in his dormitory simple phrases in Cantonese. They readily agreed and he explained that '*puk gai*' was a friendly greeting, the Chinese equivalent of '*hello*', and '*ham gaa can*' meant '*how are you today?*' Soon the small boys in his dormitory were practising the phrases with him and trying them out on their friends in other Houses. They even explained to the puzzled staff just what they meant.

It was not long before one of these English boys, full of confidence in his new linguistic skill, decided to try out his Cantonese on Brian. After tea, he sat down next to him in the Day Room to do his Prep. '*Puk gai*', he said with a grin. '*Han goo can?*'

Brian reacted immediately. He hit the boy right between the eyes, knocking him off the bench. Standing over him, Brian produced a torrent of furious Cantonese. The boy recovered enough to jump up and soon two small boys were knocking hell out of each other, punching and kicking, surrounded by the rest of the House split between those egging them on and those trying to stop the fight. Eventually the member of staff in charge of Prep grabbed Brian and the largest of the other boarders sat on the boy he had struck.

'What on earth do you think you're doing?' the staff member asked them.

'He attacked me...... without any warning..... I'm going to get him,' spluttered the other boy.

'He insulted me.........and my family...,' insisted Brian.

'What did he say?' asked the member of staff. 'Why did you get so angry, Brian?'

'He said '*drop dead*' in my language and '*may your whole family drop dead*'. I have never been so insulted and I will not speak to him again.'

During all the commotion, David quietly slipped out of Prep to visit the boys' toilets, well satisfied with his first and last attempt to teach anyone Cantonese.

Although Brian was keen on football and enjoyed playing in his House team, David much preferred books to sport. The PE Department soon discovered that he would do anything to get out of games lessons. After missing many sessions through lost kit, sore stomachs and urgent visits to the Sick Bay, he was told to report to the PE Office after House Assembly. When his friends heard this, the general view was '*David, you're dead!*'

185

To make sure he went, his Tutor took him across to the PE Office to face the full force of the PE Dept., the Head of PE flanked by the Head of Boys Games and the Head of Girls Games. It was the sporting equivalent of a visit to Star Chamber or an interrogation as terrifying as 'When did you last see your father?' David was 4ft 0ins, the Head of PE, 6ft 7ins. Even sitting down behind the desk, he towered over the Chinese boy's head. David did not lack courage, even if his sense of tact was not well developed. Any other boy would have given in at once.

'So why don't you want to come to PE lessons, David?' asked the Head of PE in a quiet but firm voice.

David stood as tall as he could, took a deep breath and looked the Head of PE in the eye, or rather looked straight at the whistle dangling in the middle of the Head of PE's chest.

'In Hong Kong,' he said, 'only stupid people do the sports.'

There was a sharp collective intake of breath and a stunned silence from the three on the other side of the desk. The Head of PE also took a deep breath as his face began to turn a rich shade of purple.

'Does that mean, David, that you think PE teachers are also stupid?' asked the Head of PE.

David had obviously thought of that.

'Oh no Sir, my father told me to respect our teachers,' he said with a very serious look. 'They are our fathers and mothers and we should respect them always. You teach me Geography and Miss Jones tries to teach me French but I am not good.'

The Head of PE had met his match. In the end a compromise was agreed. David would go to PE lessons, always carrying a book to read. As soon as he was old enough, he would start a Referees' course. Meanwhile, he would be allowed to run the touchline waving a flag. In the summer, he became one of the best cricket scorers the School had ever had and rapidly progressed to the 1st XI, travelling to away matches as both team mascot and statistician. Best of all, he proved invaluable to the PE department as the student who put all their records onto spread-sheets. Honour and respect were satisfied and David's PE reports never mentioned him missing lessons again.

~

Over the time we had at Wymondham, I made several trips to Hong Kong to recruit boarders for the College and one year, Jenny came with me to help with processing the applications. The numbers of overseas boarders never rose above about 8%, far lower than the proportion in many independent boarding schools. For us they were both a very useful way of filling empty beds and a real enriching of our College community as most proved to be very good students. As the numbers of boarders from Hong Kong built up, word got across to the other European enclave in the South China Sea, the island of Macau, then still a Portuguese Overseas Territory.

While in Hong Kong one year, Jenny and I went across to spend two days in Macau meeting prospective pupils and their parents. On the second evening, we decided to enjoy a meal together before catching the hovercraft back to Hong Kong. Relaxing in the last of the sunshine on the dining terrace of the *Pousada de Sao Tiago,* we both thought, 'what on earth are we doing here?'

The hotel was built in the ruins of the Fort from which the Portuguese had controlled their most Eastern outpost. Their settlement was the first of all the European colonies in China, and it had become the last. Just before the start of the new millennium, the Portuguese handed Macau back to the Chinese much as the British had handed back Hong Kong, but many of the ethnic Chinese residents of Macau still held Portuguese passports and still made money in their casino businesses.

After supper, we sipped our coffee and watched the junks glide past down the Xijang River as the sun set over mainland China. The simple answer to our question was that we were there to interview applicants for boarding places and to meet parents of existing students. Macau parents had discovered UK maintained boarding just as their contemporaries in Hong Kong had done a year or two earlier. It was a little more complicated as there were no British passport holders in Macau, but there were many with full Portuguese EU passports. From our point of view, these were in some ways even better. Under the Treaty of Rome, EU citizens could access boarding places in UK schools and the only charge was for boarding. Nothing in the Treaty specified that EU citizens had to live in Europe.

So we were in Macau at the invitation of parents who wanted us to meet their sons and daughters, but mainly their daughters. All were bilingual, in Cantonese and Portuguese, all spoke good English and some had a few other languages. Their parents were affluent business families rather than members of a civil service. Many had encouraged their children to learn classical instruments or to develop their artistic talents as they made their successful way through Macau's private schools. So our Macau connection produced a small but steady supply of delightful young people, with linguistic talents and interests in the arts which countered the Hong Kong Chinese stereotype of proficiency in mathematics and science. Although the Government of China did not contribute to their UK education, it was money made in the casinos, hotels and restaurants of Macau that helped to keep our boarding budget healthy.

~

The number of applicants from European Union Countries did slowly increase as parents exercised their right to access UK school places. At first, they came mainly from Holland and German. More recently they have come from the states of the former Eastern Europe, from the Czech Republic and the Baltic States, Estonia, Latvia, Lithuania. Some State Boarding schools have developed strong contacts with schools and colleges in Slovenia, Romania, Bulgaria, Poland, Croatia, Hungary and Sweden.

Now that the Baltic States and the countries of former Eastern Europe have all developed an affluent middle class, some are very interested in the opportunity for their sons and daughters to spend a year or two in an English school with a free school places and a boarding fee one third that of an independent school. Wymondham College has a link with the Czech Republic. Many other State Boarding schools are providing boarding places for these 'new Europeans' especially at 6th Form level. Many of these students have some family link with the UK, such as the grand-daughter of a Lincolnshire GP who holds a Czech Republic/EU passport and is now boarding in Market Rasen.

Meanwhile, at Wymondham, and many other SBSA schools, the international theme has hugely enriched the lives of all boarders. Once a year at the College, groups of students from all over the world were invited to organise an 'International Evening', each group providing dishes from their national cuisine which all could sample and enjoy. Some dressed in their National Costume and welcomed 'visitors', staff and other students, with greetings in their own language and an offer of a national dish. It was a wonderful celebration of the diversity of humanity, brought together by their shared experience in a UK State Boarding school. All had to be bearers of UK or EU passports, but within this envelope it was extraordinary how many different cultures of origin could be celebrated.

This diversity influenced every aspect of College life. Each Sunday in term-time, the boarders and staff met for a service in the College Chapel. The service was deliberately made as inclusive as possible within a broadly Protestant Christian framework. For example, we invited boarders to join us in the Lord's Prayer if they wished to; we did not simply say 'Let us pray'.

On Remembrance Sunday, we met for worship in a WWII Nissen Hut which once housed wounded or sick young American flyers. In the decades and centuries before WWII, their fore-fathers had come from many different European, African, American and Asian cultures to build the United States of America. They had come to Norfolk to fight for the freedom of the West against the German and Italian Nazi evil which was trying to dominate Europe, and they had suffered for that cause. But many German, Italian and Japanese families had also suffered in that conflict. Our Remembrance service had to reflect that as we had boarders from Germany and from Japan alongside the British, Dutch and Chinese in our boarding houses. It was always a very moving service as we remembered together, all who had died and we were all the richer for that experience.

There will be those who question why a school in England with all teaching and learning costs funded by the British tax payer should be allowed to admit students from EU countries. The answer is of course that the Treaty of Rome opens up this opportunity as a reciprocal arrangement. Children of British parents who happen to be resident in France or Italy or any other EU state can be admitted to the schools which that state provides for its own citizens, without charge.

As there are very many more British citizens resident with their families in the Dordogne, in the south of Spain and in regions of Italy popular with the British, than there are beds available for EU boarders in England's SBSA schools, the balance of financial advantage is heavily in favour of the British tax-payer. From the SBSA school's point of view, having a minority of overseas boarders from EU states or from Hong Kong and Macau helps to ensure that their boarding houses remain viable.

14. Teachers, Tutors and Inspectors

Boarding schools need good buildings, but they don't make a good boarding school. As all Heads of boarding schools knew, they depend on good teachers. They need young graduates, often in their first posts, who are prepared to be 'on duty' to ensure good order and safety in the boarding house. Even more, they need experienced and capable senior teachers, prepared to live and work often with their families in the boarding houses they lead. Young and not so young these teaching staff often live in, accepting the limitations of a bed-sitting room or small flat in a boarding house and free meals as a reasonable price for an intensive and demanding life during term-time.

Boarding schools could not function without House Tutors, young men and women prepared to share the supervision of boarders with senior staff. Teachers who undertake these House Tutor roles seldom stay long. My own time in the role at King's, Worcester was two years. That is about the norm and it works well. Young graduates move on after an intensive induction into working with young people into more responsible roles in boarding houses or find their future in leadership roles within their own subject. Few leave teaching altogether. They contribute their energy, enthusiasm and up-to-date knowledge of both their subject and university life to the school community and they are much closer in age and attitude to their 6th Form pupils than the more senior members of staff. At Wymondham, we needed to recruit House Tutors from applicants for teaching posts every year and it was part of the boarding culture of the College that all teaching staff made some contribution to the supervision of boarders in the houses. To make this clear in contracts of employment was essential and this was one of the issues which we were criticised for when an Ofsted team came to inspect the College in 1994. They simply did not understand how boarding schools operated.

At that time, State Boarding schools were inspected as if they were state schools which just happened to have a majority of pupils who did not go home at four o'clock. Teams of inspectors showed little interest in what happened after the school teaching day and no interest in what happened at the weekends, both of which were very important parts of the life of a large boarding school. Our Governors did their best to encourage the Inspection Team to understand our boarding school culture but it was simply outside the professional experience of any of them. All had taught in day schools and several had led departments or year groups in such schools. None had ever worked in a boarding school, independent or day.

When the Governors learnt of this, they demanded a meeting with the Lead Inspector. Under pressure to tell them just what experience she did have which made her able to make judgements on Europe's largest state boarding school, she said that she had once visited Oakham School as a friend of a parent with a son there. The Governors were reduced to incredulity, but there was little they could do. To be fair to the Team, at that time, Ofsted contracts did not include any time for an effective inspection of boarding and we just had to get on with it.

When the report was published the College was described as 'satisfactory'. This seemed to us to be damning with faint praise. Our results had started to improve, as was our popularity amongst parents considering applying for places for their children. We were said to have just 1% of pupils on free school meals, which was true for day pupils having a free College lunch on the national scheme. It completely ignored the fact that 20% of our five hundred boarders received free breakfast, lunch, tea and supper because their boarding places were financially supported by Norfolk County Council.

At the end of the inspection week, I took Assembly for the whole College as usual and let the community of over one thousand people know that we were 'satisfactory'. They and I wanted to be 'good', and in some ways 'the best'. We knew that we were not that yet, but we also knew that we could be. I promised the College that if any of them ever caught me writing 'satisfactory' on any report, they had my full permission to complain to me, the staff, the Governors and to Ofsted.

If Ofsted failed to understand the way in which our Tutors worked in both the classroom and the boarding house, they were even more incapable of understanding the real pillars of the College community, the senior teachers who were also in charge of each of the six boarding houses. These key colleagues were responsible for all the boarders and day pupils in their houses. At Wymondham, we called them Head of House, a name usually reserved in the independent sector for the most senior prefect but I wanted to emphasise that we were different. 'Housemasters and Housemistresses' seemed unnecessarily clumsy so 'Heads of House' they stayed, running their part of the school community with much of the responsibilities of a Headteacher delegated to each of them. I have known and worked with many Heads of House whose dedication to their House was an inspiration to younger colleagues and a source of huge confidence for parents.

Chris was one like that, the Head of a large community of over a hundred boarders, boys and girls from twelve to seventeen who shared their House with another eighty day pupils. He knew every boy and every girl, their strengths and weaknesses, their interests and what made them bored. He and his wife shared their small flat with their two daughters, living right at the heart of his house. His team of tutors and matrons always had his support and they in turn were devoted both to Chris and to the students in his house.

To lead his house and to teach at all levels in the school might seem enough for one man, but Chris was involved in two other major activities. With a local policeman, he ran the most effective drugs education programme I have ever come across. This involved training a team of teenagers to be able to offer 'peer-counselling' to the other students of the school. Part of their training was to be taken by Chris in the minibus to the local Category C Prison. They would be taken through initial search and admission barriers, through all the locked doors and onto the wing. There a team of prisoners had agreed to talk to these young people about the impact which drug-taking had had on their lives, the lives of their wives and children and the communities from which they had come. It was an overwhelmingly powerful experience. As one of the boys who took part said, it was the best drugs education experience that he had ever had.

Chris had yet another passion. He was very interested in military aircraft and in working with a team of students on restoring parts of historic aircraft on loan from the Imperial War Museum at Duxford. So successful was this that he decided to ask Duxford to lend his team a full airframe for restoration. In 1993, one of the last remaining T22 Sea Vampires held in the Duxford collection arrived at the

College in sections on a large low-loader. Over the next three years, Chris' Aircraft Restoration Group cleaned, repaired, repainted and re-assembled this entire aircraft ready for it to be returned to Duxford to form part of the permanent aircraft display there. It is still there as part of the National Collection.

At the other end of the College campus, Malcolm led his House with the same distinction as Chris. He too lived in a small Head of House flat with his wife and their two children, inspired a team of tutors and matrons to treat their boarding and day pupils with the same respect that Malcolm showed them. His passions were PE and singing, both activities which the College encouraged through inter-House competitions. Malcolm was one of those teachers who could work with under-confident young people and make it possible for them to achieve levels of success that they never dreamt of, not just in sport and music but in all their College work.

Every year, after all the Christmas parties had become a distant memory, we would come back in the New Year and all the houses would go into frantic preparations for the 'Mair Cup'. This was the annual College inter-house music competition, set up in 1967 in memory of a former Head of Music. Each house had to prepare three items, one a showcase for individual or small group musical talent and one for a small and expert choir. The third item was an opportunity for as many of the House as could be persuaded to sing to provide a musical spectacular, a celebration of energy, emotion and glorious song. Through the early 1990s, Chris's house won the Mair Cup four times, goading Malcolm into such total domination of the competition that his house won it for seven years in a row, and then a further

196

five times before Malcolm moved on from the College. Such was the rivalry between them that dark mutterings were heard about the allocation of the Y7 entrants to the College with musical talent to one house or the other.

These two men were superb Heads of house and we were very fortunate to have women of the same stature as leaders of boarding communities. Gail served as the Head of the 6th Form house for many years, always offering expert advice for university applications, always effective when one of her charges stepped out of line. She was almost impossible to distract from her quiet insistence on the highest standards of courtesy and consideration for others in the House. She must many times have been in despair over the idiotic behaviour of some of her students and have had to cover for members of staff who forgot to turn up for their duties, but she never showed it. Like a serene swan, Gail always maintained a calm exterior however frantically she was paddling under water. The most senior students recognised in Gail an ally and a friend. Many remained in touch with her long after they had left us.

We had many other key players in our team of Heads of House, each contributing their own strengths, but the one whose contribution was critical to our future took charge of the new arrangements in Peel. We could recruit as many 11 year old girls and boys as possible but they had to settle happily into boarding in Peel if we were going to survive as a boarding school. Fortunately, we found in Heather the ideal person for the job. She and her husband had worked in residential care in the City of Leeds which must have been a very challenging introduction to looking after very needy young men. She taught Home Economics for a number of years as it morphed into Food Technology before she came to the College.

When first she became Malcolm's Deputy Head of House, Heather lived in a small flat with her husband and their two sons. When she applied for the Headship of the new Y7 House, she had little difficulty in persuading the governors that she had all the skills and personal qualities she would need to make it a success. She handled some very sad cases of children who had been deeply damaged by their family background. Most of them flourished in her care. She also led a team of tutors and GAP-year volunteers from all over the world to create a warm and secure home for our youngest boarders. Their parents sung her praises.

When Ofsted next visited us in 1998, we were much better prepared. We had sorted out our terms of service for staff and reviewed all salary scales so that teaching staff were well rewarded for the extra responsibilities they carried in the boarding houses. Just before the inspection I had an enquiry from a Housemaster at Eton College.

'Would you be willing to advise our Headmaster and the College bursar of the salary scale on which Wymondham pays your Heads of House?' he enquired politely.

I was of course pleased to be helpful and when the figures were compared with what Eton paid their senior staff, the rumour that Wymondham College paid more, was clearly true!

'Of course we pay more', I told them. 'Our houses are much bigger than yours. They have both boys and girls. They actually work longer terms and lead larger teams of staff tutors – of course they earn more!'

Whether the Eton Housemasters managed to use our figures to persuade their Head and Bursar to increase their salaries I never learnt. Such matters were said to be 'confidential', but it was the start of a link between the two Colleges which has developed ever since.

The 1998 Ofsted team did understand us as a boarding community, did stay into the evenings and even stayed over the weekend. When the Bishop of Lynn came to conduct a confirmation service in our College Chapel, his service was 'observed' by the member of the inspection team responsible for *'pupils' spiritual, moral, social and cultural development'*. Needless to say, the Bishop got a very good Ofsted grade for his sermon, possibly the only Church of England Bishop to have received such an accolade!

When the 1998 Ofsted report was published, there was much celebration. Wymondham College received the highest possible grade overall and we appeared in the Chief Inspector's Annual Report as one of the outstanding schools of 1998. A small boy in Y9 grinned at me on the way into Assembly.

'We did all right, Sir, didn't we?' he said – indeed we did!

Some of the information which we provided for the inspection team proved difficult to explain.

'How many feeder schools do you have?' I was asked.

'173,' I replied.

'That's not possible', said the Lead Inspector. 'That must be the number of 6th Formers.'

'No,' I said. 'That's the number of feeder schools. Our current boarding and day pupils come from all over Norfolk, all over the UK and many from overseas – one hundred and seventy three different schools, world-wide.' 'I see,' he said.

Then we talked about unauthorised and authorised absence. 'Why were our figures so much lower than the County and National averages?'

199

'Could it have something to do with three factors?' I surmised. 'Firstly, our pupils actually like being here and if they are ever ill, they are still here because as boarders they stay here in our Sick-Bay – still present. Secondly, their parents have to bring them here and have also paid boarding or day-boarding fees. We don't give a rebate for time missed through absence so parents have a major incentive to ensure that they do come to school. Lastly, we lock them all in every night and that does wonders for our attendance figures!'

He looked at me and began to understand that we really were a very unusual school.

~

Not all our staff were as successful as our best House Tutors and Heads of House. Sometimes sadly, House Tutors got stuck. They had chosen to live in school accommodation and with a rapidly escalating housing market found themselves priced out of accommodation outside the school. One or two found the pressure of sharing life with large numbers of adolescents wore them out and occasionally sought escape in the local pub or in a can or bottle in the privacy of their own rooms. Boarding house life is not for the fragile.

Teaching staff who also work in school boarding houses are subject to other temptations, although illicit liaisons within the house with individual boarders with whom they share their lives is unlikely to be one of them. If you are tempted to conduct a relationship with an under-age or post-16 pupil, there are much more discrete places to do so than in a House Tutor's flat surrounded by boarders and with sole access past their dormitories. Any professional teacher who gets involved in such a relationship has only himself, or occasionally herself, to blame when a promising teaching career comes to an abrupt and inevitable end.

Sometimes, teachers just take their duty of being '*in loco parentis*' too far. Teachers of subjects which had a high proportion of coursework as part of the GCSE or other examinations were particularly vulnerable, and it was a relief when course work was reduced at GCSE. At one time, an English GCSE grade could be awarded by the Examination Board after the candidate had submitted a portfolio of written work which was first graded by the teacher, without any external written examination. This was 100% Course Work assessment. The members of staff of the school would meet to agree grade boundaries and then have their work 'moderated' by an external examiner who sampled the folders of work and confirmed the validity of the grades awarded. Many teachers were concerned that they had little means of telling what work was solely that of the candidate and what had been 'helped', 'drafted' or even simply written by the candidate's parents or other contacts out of school time.

Boarders whose English work was assessed in this way could not of course get much help from their parents except at weekends or during the holidays, but there were adults in the school who could help, especially House Tutors. Such teachers may even feel that they have a duty to help boarders, to make up for the loss of their parents' help. After all, they may argue, day pupils have an unfair advantage.

The first staff disciplinary issue I faced as the Head of a boarding school was a dispute between an English teacher and his Head of Department. The teacher was also the boarding house Tutor for some of the pupils in his Y11 English class. His colleagues were sure that he had gone well beyond the allowed role of the teacher in assessing his pupils' course work. They refused to agree his grades and alleged that he had 'improved' early drafts of work to ensure that higher grades could be awarded. He then awarded higher grades. He denied any improper conduct. I walked into a situation where my predecessor had suspended a teacher for improperly enhancing course-work and then, when two competing Teaching Unions became involved, he had to suspend the Head of Department for making unfounded allegations.

I consulted the Examination Board and it soon became clear that the interpretation of what was permissible for teachers assessing English Course-work was very vague. The Board advised me that it was almost impossible to make a case for disciplinary action against a teacher on the grounds of improper involvement in Course-work. The Board just did not want to know. The conflict was clearly getting no-where, so both were allowed to return to teaching on the clear understanding that the House Tutor had received a written instruction from me that he must not in any way discuss or assist in the English course-work of any pupil he taught while he was also on duty in the boarding House.

The temptation to ensure that his pupils got good grades proved too strong. The next time his Head of Department came to see me, he had a file from a boy who had been very grateful to the House Tutor for a great deal of help. A quick check of the duty rosters confirmed that this had been during Prep supervised by his English teacher. So the teacher was suspended again and when the case came before the Governors' Staff Discipline Panel, even his own Union representative agreed with the outcome. He had to go, in what is called an agreed end of contract. I wrote a statement giving the facts about his length of service at the College with no comment on the quality of that service. He left our staff. It still seems ironic to me that the issue over which he lost his job was not the blatant way in which he had as an English Teacher improved his pupils' course work himself before awarding a higher grade, but his clear disobedience of a reasonable instruction given by his Principal.

~

There is another model for staffing boarding houses – the non-teaching house parent. Combining the role of teacher and house tutor makes huge demands on individuals and boarding houses need other responsible adults who are not working in both the house and the classroom. Children who find school difficult, for whatever reason, can sometimes relate more easily to concerned adults who are not teachers. Most boarding school houses today have a team of both teaching and non-teaching staff covering the necessary supervision duties and are the better for this. There are some houses which are managed exclusively by 'House Parents', men and women who undertake a boarding supervision role as their sole focus and many are very effective. It can be a very rewarding and relatively well-paid job. One house has a former 6th Form student who enjoyed boarding, completed his University degree and then returned to the boarding house as a full-time Housemaster, without a teaching commitment because he very much enjoyed working with the boarders.

It is still true that most parents who send their children to boarding schools seem to prefer to relate to professional teachers but good house staff can also inspire parental confidence and have a lot more time and energy than most teachers at the end of the school day. However, most boarding schools need to recruit some teachers who are prepared to do boarding duties and maintaining the supply of good graduate teachers is vital to the quality of schools.

16. Boarding Parents

Parental choice of school brought our boarders to Wymondham College as even those who were supported by public funds always had a choice and had to apply to us, rather than any other of the hundreds of English boarding schools, independent and state. Those who came as day students also had to apply as the College had no catchment area, places being allocated in order of proximity to the College. Sometimes, we got into a dispute with parents over their wish to be given a day place for their child – usually because their idea of 'proximity' clashed with ours. One parent who took the College Governors to court over the admission of his son lost his case. They had refused to accept that he and his son lived in a chicken shed. The fact that the shed was in a field on his large Norfolk farm and marginally closer to the College than the home occupied by a successful applicant for a day place was judged irrelevant.

Occasionally, we had to say to the parent who wanted his or her child to come to us as a boarder that we did not think this was a good idea. No parent could 'make' their child become a boarder and we always made sure that the child had at least been consulted and had agreed to come, even if it was not at first their own idea. Very, very rarely, we lost a boarder because they were really unhappy in boarding.

Nearly all of our parents were hugely supportive of the College, volunteering to help at fund-raising events, serving as Governors and members of the Parents-Staff Association. They acted as our advocates in all the social networks not just of Norfolk but of all of East Anglia, the Armed Forces and in their particular community overseas. It was our parents who had saved the College from closure in 1986. It was our parents who sent us the pupils to help us to ensure that our examination results climbed steadily through the 1990s.

But not all of these parents were easy to work with. Some tested me and my colleagues to the limit. With some, we never established a good relationship. Of the six girls in that A dormitory of twelve year olds, it was Hannah, or rather her mother, that proved to be the most demanding.

It was three in the morning when the 'phone beside my bed in the Principal's house rang. Struggling to wake up, I put the light on and picked up the 'phone.

'Mr Haden here,' I said, 'who's calling?'

A voice not unlike the late Queen Mother's came on the line.

'This is Mrs H-J and I'm 'phoning about an urgent problem. Hannah has just phoned me in floods of tears because she has lost her pink furry pencil case.'

'I'm sorry, could you repeat that?' I said unsure that I was not still dreaming.

'I shall repeat it as many times as you like, Principal, my Hannah has lost her pink furry pencil case, and has phoned me to say how unhappy she is. I want to know what you are going to do about it. Do you now understand?'

I understood all too well. Hannah had returned to her boarding house after the Christmas holiday showing all her friends her new tablet 'phone. She explained to them that it was a 'tri-band' and would work anywhere in the world. She could use it to 'phone her mother in Saudi Arabia, where Mrs H-J was accompanying her husband who was busy helping to train pilots in the Royal Saudi Air Force.

'Mrs H-J,' I said, trying to sound civil if not actually pleased to be woken up. 'Do you realise what the time is here? It's three in the morning!'

'Of course I know what the time is; Hannah has just told me. She cannot sleep because she's lost her pencil case. She's really worried that she'll be in trouble in Maths because she won't have her geometry instruments in period three. Do you think that very plain girl in her dormitory has stolen it? I need you to sort this out, Headmaster, because I am very busy this week entertaining the Saudi officers' wives and I simply cannot cope with Hannah's distressing 'phone calls.'

'Mrs H-J,' I said, now fully awake and remembering our previous conversations. 'I fully understand that it is distressing for you to get 'phone calls from Hannah when she loses things, but I doubt very much that the item has been stolen. She has probably left it somewhere, just as she lost her new hockey stick and her new calculator, both of which the staff found for her. We'll do our best to help her in the morning. Now can I please go back to sleep?'

'Principal, you will I am sure remember telling us that the College always tries to work with parents and children. How are we supposed to help you to do that if we cannot keep in touch? But I do understand, it is a little early with you. It's a lovely day here. Good bye, Principal.'

With that, she rang off and I turned off the light.

~

Hannah's mother clearly thought that one of the girls in her 'dorm' was likely to be a thief because she came from a much less affluent background than her daughter. We had to work hard to convince such families that their children would actually benefit from the social mix of the College.

The truth is that irresponsible parenting and badly behaved children are not exclusive to poor communities. It is certainly much harder to bring up children to become good citizens if all the members of the surrounding community lack a strong moral framework. But this is not exclusive to poor communities. Many who would see themselves as part of the comfortable middle classes, can be equally irresponsible. The father whose easily accessed cannabis supply had ensured that his son forfeited his College place was not the one who got the blame, but it was his fault.

~

Another very good example of irresponsible parenting was the case of the boarder who shot the Head of Maths – or rather, that's what the girl who told her House Head about it claimed he had done.

At the end of morning school one day, the Head of Maths was walking home across the tennis courts when he thought he heard a 'thwack' noise and felt a tap on his shoulder through his padded car-coat. He had no idea what this meant and walked on home, unconcerned.

Shortly afterwards, two frightened girls appeared at the House office and asked to see their Head of House.

'Sir, Sir,' they told him. 'We think they've shot Mr J. on the tennis courts.'

'What do you mean?' he'd asked. 'Is Mr Jones hurt?' 'No, he's fine', they said, 'but you need to stop them shooting at people.'

That seemed to him to be urgently true. He went into the Day Room with the girls. All seemed normal. The boys and girls were gathering before moving as a group to have their lunch in the Dining Hall. The member of staff on duty had just finished calling the roll and giving out notices when we walked in. He explained why two of the girls were late because they had been to see him, and suggested that the House should go to lunch with Matron, while he came across to see me.

He explained what the girls had said. I looked completely puzzled.

'How could someone be shooting the Head of Maths on the tennis courts without any one, except for two 15 year old girls, noticing?'

'I've no idea', he said, 'but that's what they said. The courts are just next to my House and the only place that you could shoot someone who was walking across them would be from the top floor, on the Boys' Side.'

While the boarders were in lunch, we went through the boys' dormitories and found what we were looking for under the duvet of a bed in the Boys Y10 dorm. It was a ball-bearing gun, a replica AK47 rifle. The box was still under the bed.

'*High quality, durable and accurate BB rifle, a great training aid for improving your marksmanship and gun handling – bullet proof glasses inside*' was printed in large letters across the top. In much smaller print below, there was a warning. '*Do not shoot at any humans or animals.*'

We were appalled at what we had found. We quickly put it in a black bin bag and took it down to the house office. We knew whose bed it had been found in. As soon as he came back from lunch, the Duty Master brought him into the office where we sat behind the desk. The gun and its box were concealed in the bin bag on the desk.

'Sit down, Stephen, we need to talk to you. We've just searched your dorm and found something under the duvet on your bed. Do you want to tell us about?'

Stephen looked very worried.

'It's the BB gun, isn't it, Sir?' he blurted out, and the whole stupid story poured out.

He was in the U16 cricket team and he had gone to play another school. Before the match, his parents had arranged to come to watch him and for him to visit a family friend whose son was also at the College, 'to give him a break before the exams'. They would return him to the school on Sunday evening. It was all planned, agreed and above board. What they did not know was that the two boys had also planned to meet up with an older friend, an 'uncle', to go into the town. There the 'uncle' would buy BB guns for both of them, at £29.95 for replica AK47s. The guns were readily available to anyone over 18. Stephen had put his at the bottom of his cricket bag, enjoyed his evening at his friend's home and come back to school as planned.

Stephen claimed that he had intended to leave the gun in its box and to take it home at Half Term. But one of the other boys in his dormitory had seen the box and pleaded to be allowed to look at the gun itself. Temptation proved too strong. Stephen had shown them how the gun worked by firing out of the window at a pigeon. He missed the pigeon but the boys were very impressed.

'There's some reinforced glass on the landing,' one of them said. 'I wonder if it's bullet-proof? Shall we see if the ball-bearing will go through that?'

They tried and it did, leaving a neat entry hole and a conical exit 'wound' on the other side.

Stephen said he wanted to stop then and to put the gun away, but just as he was doing so, the Head of Maths walked across the tennis courts in full view below the dormitory window.

'Bet you can't hit him,' goaded one of the boys.

'I could try with the telescopic sight, but it's probably too far,' said Stephen, pushing the gun carefully through the open window.

The Head of Maths did notice the 'thwack' of Stephen's 20g plastic pellet hitting his padded coat but did not see the boys at the open window. It was two girls walking past that heard the 'thwack', spotted Stephen and his gun at the open window and ran to report what they had seen.

Stephen's parents were distraught when they came to pick him, and the gun, up.

'We never knew he had it and no-one actually got hurt.'

But even they could see that firing a gun at a teacher was bound to be an exclusion offence in any school, and they did not challenge the decision. The really sad thing was that a boy who enjoyed boarding and was doing well in every way blew his chances, thanks to an adult who took no responsibility for the gun he bought for him or for the fact that he let him bring it back to school.

~

Independent schools quite rightly pride themselves on their culture of courtesy to parents, especially parents visiting the school. Good manners are important when you are trying to attract paying customers and that is equally true for those of us in State Boarding schools when we welcome parents and their children to our Open Days. But there are some visitors who are not welcome.

In 1996, Heads received guidance from the Government on how best to deal with unwanted and abusive adults on school premises. The legislation made clear that Heads could arrange for such adults to remove themselves from school premises or refer the matter to the Police. Little did I think that shortly afterwards I would find myself following such welcome advice in a very unexpected context.

It was always good to see parents at the matches on the school field, but there had been problems with over-enthusiastic fathers supporting their sons playing in school matches.

One of the local independent schools was playing our U16 XV on our field with a posse of supporting fathers on the touch line. One of our PE staff was acting as referee and it was a finely balanced match. One of the visiting fathers was getting more and more frustrated with his son's inability to break through our boys' heroic defence.

'Come on, John, get stuck in and fight for it,' he shouted. 'Get that boy and flatten him....etc.' Then he switched to an attack on the ref. 'Are you blind, ref? That's a knock on; blow your whistle man!'

The referee, one of our PE staff, came across to the touch-line and had a word with the parent, to his evident anger. Once the match was started again, the abuse continued.

'That's not in straight!'..... 'Clear obstruction!'..... 'Why don't you do something about it?'

The ref came across to the touch-line again and had a word with me.

'It's no good,' he said. 'The boys are getting really upset about these comments and I'll have to stop the match.'

I said I would have a word with the visiting parent.

The next time he offered his advice to the ref, I was standing next to him.

'Excuse me, could I have a word please?'

He looked startled. 'And who are you?'

'I'm the Head of this school.'

'And I'm the Mother Superior!' he said laughing.

'You may be, but I really am the Head. I have to warn you that if there is any more abuse, the ref will stop the game. But there is another option.'

'What's that?' he said with a sneer.

'I could ask you to leave the school site', I advised him.

Five minutes later, he started again. I turned to him and said, 'I did warn you, now I am telling you. Will you please leave this school site, now?'

'What do you mean?' he said, 'I've come to support my boy and how will he get home?'

'That's fine,' I said. 'You can take him home with you.'

We did lose the match, narrowly, but it ended in good spirits. Next morning I had a 'phone call from the visiting school's Head. He had heard from his staff of my 'conversation' with one of his parents at the match.

'I just called to apologise for his behaviour and to say that maybe we should all have the guts to do what you did,' he said. 'That way we might have a chance of teaching the boys what was acceptable.'

'Maybe,' I said, 'but we don't have to treat parents as customers in quite the same way as some schools have to. But thanks for the support!'

17. Sex and Health Education

Mixed boarding schools with hundreds of hormonal young people living in close proximity will all have to face the possibility of teenage pregnancies. One well known English Public School made the national newspapers recently when an internal email was leaked to the Press. It had come from one Housemaster to all the other House Staff, copied to all Matrons, expressing anxiety about sex in school. One of the girls had been overheard claiming that the medical centre had run out of emergency contraceptive pills after a particularly busy weekend of activity.

Sex at home was one thing; sex in school was strictly forbidden. Yet pupils had claimed that they were doing it in school. The instruction to all staff was – be much more vigilant. Patrol the House more. Don't leave young people in public areas without supervision. Then someone bothered to check and discovered that the medical centre routinely carried a stock of just two such pills; the collapse of moral standards seemed much less dramatic. Anxiety levels dropped, but it was still worrying.

~

The challenge of providing effective sex education for schools has been a perennial priority. When I became one of three Deputy Heads in the 14-18 school in Northallerton, it was agreed that we should have a programme of 'Personal, Social and Health Education' for all students from the age of fourteen. Agreeing was one thing, actually providing it was another. As I had the job of drawing up the school time table, I tried to get volunteers to cover the 'Health' modules of this course, but with little success. The Head of Year 11, who also taught Girls' PE, thought it a very good idea. She might be willing to help. My fellow deputies, a historian and a geographer, thought that the Science Department was best equipped to offer the course and volunteered me on the grounds that I was a scientist! So began my career as a teacher of Sex Education alongside the Year of Year 11, the stern but understanding Miss B.

We didn't have £1000 for Health Education in our school budget so we could not afford a '*virtual infant simulator*' and no TV channel filmed our efforts to explain the joys and sorrows of having children to Year 11, but Miss B and I were proud of our efforts. We embarked on a mission to reduce the school pupil pregnancy rate to zero. Our challenge was to show them what parenthood was really like. It helped that twice over those years I was a new father with answers to their questions hot from the front line of nappies and sleeplessness. The course was technically called 'Health Education', but some of them put '*Sex with Miss B and Mr H.*' on the Thursday pm slot of their personal planners.

The centre-piece of our course was the video: '*Jenny is Born*'. We showed it every four weeks to a fresh Tutor Group in the aptly named 'circus' of PSHE, giving Jenny the shortest gestation period of any known large mammal. That video was our life-line. Forty minutes of graphic images and sounds of labour, with the final triumphant look on her mother's face as Jenny wailed for the first time. There was then just enough time for some of the best discussions I've ever had with 16 year olds. Even after the film had been shown for four years, it still had the power to reduce teenagers to silent wonder and amazement at the miracle of birth.

But we had more to do. There was a knock on the office door. It was a 6th Form deputation, bored with 'private study'.

'Sir, instead of all this citizenship stuff, can we do what you do with Miss B. on Thursday afternoons?'

This could be tricky.

Then one of them said 'You know Sir, watch the film.' All became clear. So I consulted Miss B. Should we move our mission up to the sophisticated levels of Year 12? She, being a PE specialist, had seen student reaction to carnage on the hockey and rugby fields. Surely they would cope with the blood and obvious agonies of childbirth.

It was a disaster. At first, the dodgy red/green control on the TV reduced the image to a discrete grey, and they began to relax. But when the old TV warmed up and the screen started to head for pink, they all went ominously silent. The first boy fainted even before the baby's head was engaged. We were so busy dragging him out of the room that we didn't notice the screen lurching into a vivid red. By the time Jenny had arrived, half the surviving boys were hiding behind their A level text books and most of the girls had decided to become nuns.

'A bit late,' was Miss B.'s knowing comment.

So we never repeated '*what you and Miss B. do on Thursdays*' with 6th Form Tutor groups. The Citizenship teacher reported that, after our 'little experiment', Year 12 seemed much more willing to listen to him droning on about the importance of taking an active part........... in Politics.

~

When we moved from Northallerton to Louth, I found it equally difficult to recruit volunteers to teach the Health Education course that was clearly needed as much in

Lincolnshire as it had been in North Yorkshire. Having left Miss B behind, I needed a new ally. Fortunately a new School Nursing Sister had just taken up the role in Louth and she was a strong advocate of 'Well Women' clinics which seemed to focus on 'self-examination'. She was very happy to take her message into schools and '*Sister R. and the Head*' were soon established as the team who delivered Health and Sex Education to Year 10 in the PSHE 'circus'. All seemed to be going well and, she was certainly pleased with our efforts, but she asked me to find out what the students thought of the course. It did not seem appropriate for the Head to call in a sample of Year 10 to ask for some feed-back but I did get to overhear conversations over school dinners by sitting at the boarders' tables. They soon got so used to you being around that they forgot you were there.

'So......' asked Cristobel, who had plans to be the next size-zero supermodel and was picking at the edges of her tuna salad. She had missed period 4 to go to a Counselling session which no-one was supposed to know about but which formed the subject of endless whisperings amongst the Y10 girls. '....what was Health Ed like?'

'Great,' said Sebastian, shovelling vast amounts of shepherds' pie and chips into his mouth. He played at Number 8 in the school U15 pack and had ambitions to play for the 1st XV on his way to England and the Lions. He was already well over six feet tall in Y10, with hands like dinner plates.

'We had Sister R. and she showed us her pair of silicone tits. They wobbled a bit when she passed them round and she said we should all feel them carefully and check them for lumps.'

He waggled his fingers to demonstrate the technique. 'I found a lump like a hard round bit in the side of the left hand one,' he announced with a look of triumph.

'How gross,' sneered Cristobel, her skinny arm protectively crossing her even skinnier chest. 'And I suppose you disgusting lot all enjoyed having a good feel.'

Sebastian looked affronted. 'What if we did? Sister said it's important for girls to check their breasts regularly and it's really easy to do when you're standing in front of a mirror.'

'You'd have to take your clothes off first,' said Thomas helpfully, looking lasciviously at Brenda, the Girls' U15 netball captain sitting across the table whose school blouse was struggling to keep control of her chest. 'Sister also said that husbands could help their wives by encouraging them and even checking their breasts for them if they did it very gently and lovingly.'

'Just don't try claiming to be checking for lumps next time you get caught behind the laundry room with your hands up Sam's jumper,' said Brenda with a grin. 'Anyway, boys, it'll be your turn next week.'

'What do you mean?' asked Cristobel, finally giving up on lunch and pushing her tuna salad away from her. Sebastian explained.

'Just as the bell was going, Sister showed us her balls in a canvas bag and said it was a model scrotum. She said it was easy for boys to check their balls if you did it in the bath.'

'Now that's something even you couldn't do behind the laundry rooms.' said Brenda.

'Oh, I d'know,' said Sebastian. 'You could with the right girl.'

Just as the meal was ending, he pulled the salad plate across the table. 'If you don't want your tuna, Cristobel, can I have it?'

~

When we got to Norfolk, my involvement in Health Education continued, partly because I actually found it a very good way of being involved in teaching all the Y10s and partly because no-one else was very keen to cover it. The Science Department taught the section of the Biology course which covered human reproduction, but anything which involved discussions with young people about sexual issues which concerned their own lives was beyond what they were prepared to do.

I was sure that such discussions should take place and equally sure that the Principal was probably not the best person to actually lead them. But it did have one great merit. None of the parents ever raise any issue of what we did in the Health Education module of the Y10 PSHE course with me or with any other colleague. Having me covering the material seemed to shut down all discussion of content, which saved a lot of time. I did at least meet every Y10 student in class and had a chance to get to know them better.

It was just at this time that teachers were beginning to look more closely at the results of what they did in the classroom. Departments were becoming more accountable and comparisons were beginning to be made about why some subjects always seemed to produce much more impressive grades than others. At first, there were the usual arguments for special pleading.

The German teacher tried to convince me that '*it was well known and widely accepted that German was a much more difficult language than French*' and he could not therefore be expected to match the French departments consistently excellent grades.

Eventually, under pressure from the Head of Modern Languages, he did accept that his teaching had something to do with the results and moved on to a less demanding school. His successor's German grades were soon as good as and often better than the French.

As I was technically responsible for the contraception element of the Health Education course, one staff wag suggested that my efforts should also be judged by results and demanded to know how many of our girls in Year 10 and above had ever got pregnant before they left us. Fortunately for me, this information remained with the highly discrete Sick Bay sisters and the College doctor. We certainly were not going to ask the girls or their parents to contribute to this part of the College data-base.

~

With a College site of over eighty acres, much of which was dense woodland, there were plenty of places where amorous couples could get to know each other better. One small copse lay between the Principal's House and the lights of the Sick Bay. In the winter when the leaves were off the trees, the view from our house included the bare limbs of this copse back-lit against the bright lights beyond. Occasionally, I would watch 6th Form students take an evening stroll from their boarding house into the trees, clearly assuming that they were well hidden. In summertime, they were, but come November with the leaves fallen, their trust in the cover was all too clearly misplaced. Just occasionally, when things were going a bit too well, I would take a torch and walk round to the side of the copse to wish

220

the occupants a very loud good-evening and suggest that they should get back to their books.

~

My predecessor at Wymondham had taken over a mixed boarding school with quite separate boys' and girls' houses. The two sexes met in lessons, but they kept to their own houses for meals and evening prep. He first introduced mixed dining – for boys and girls to have meals together was regarded as a major issue at first but staff and students soon got used to the idea. The next stage was more revolutionary. The boarding houses were all actually designed as two halves of a square around a small central courtyard. The two halves were at first two separate houses, either all boys or all girls.

Once mixed dining was accepted it was relatively easy to switch from two same sex houses in the same building to one boys' and one girls' or rather one overall mixed house. Each house had a boys' side and a girls' side with their own single sex staircases from the mixed ground floor. For students, there were no links between the sides on the upper floors. The staff flats, two for Tutors on the first floor and two for Matrons on the top floor, formed the barriers between the sexes. All tutors' flats had a spare bedroom for a relief tutor to use, and the matrons' flats were the same. Whenever the boarders were in their dormitories, the staff on duty overnight occupied their flats, keeping the genders apart.

For this system of mixed boarding houses to work there had to be very clear rules. The simplest was to insist that no boy ever stood even on the first step of the girls' staircase or ever even opened the door of the girls' downstairs toilets and changing rooms, and vice versa. As the students expressed it, *'if you're caught on the wrong side, you're dead.'* By 'being dead' they meant that they were sent to the Principal and their parents were required to take them home permanently. It may seem a draconian approach but it worked, and in my eight years at the College I only ever had to send one girl and one boy home for being on the wrong side.

~

But even in the best regulated boarding schools, boys and girls will quite naturally form strong relationships and sometimes, even with the best advice, things got out of hand. One couple with a daughter at the College lived about an hour's drive away, just far enough to make daily travel difficult but near enough to support their daughter's hockey matches when her team played at home. Penny loved life as a boarder. Tall and blonde, with a pretty smile and lots of friends, she sailed through her school work. All the staff thought she would get a string of A* grades on her way to the 6th Form.

Midway through Penny's Year 11, her mother 'phoned to ask if she could come to see me. She had 'something very personal' to discuss. She came in to my office clutching an envelope.

'Penny left this at home on Sunday night,' she said. 'She obviously wanted me to find it after she came back from school because she put it under her dirty washing left on the chair in her bedroom for me to collect up on Monday. I want you to read it.'

'Are you sure?' I said. 'Do you think Penny would be happy for me to see it? She's put: 'Mum and Dad' on the envelope.'

'She's my daughter and she's still only 15. I want you to know what's happened,' she said, handing me the letter.

There were several sheets of the pink paper. In her neat handwriting, Penny had written:

'Dear Mum and Dad,

I wanted to talk to you but I couldn't. I did not want to spoil a lovely weekend. But I don't know what to do. By the time you read this, I'll be back at school and they'll all be talking about me again. You said that I could go home with Richard last weekend. It was all arranged and you had said it was OK for his Mum to pick me up on Friday night. We had a great time at the Funfair on Saturday and his parents were really sweet. I think they really like me and I thought that Richard was special too.

I didn't want things to get too serious because we've both got exams this year and I thought that he understood. Then his Mum and Dad went out to play golf on Sunday and things just happened. He told me that he really loved me and I think that I loved him, then. Anyway, we ended up on his bed and it seemed OK to let him have sex. It wasn't that great although I pretended that it was. We got everything straight for when his parents got back and his Mum brought us back to school in the evening.

I'm not stupid and I knew what I was doing. Just to be sure, I saw Sickbay Sister on Sunday night and told her what had happened. She was a bit heavy with me but arranged for me to pick up a morning-after pill at the Monday morning surgery. When I got back to the House at Break everyone seemed to be looking at me. At lunchtime it was the same, although they were obviously talking about me as well. It was horrible.

I ask Lucy what they were saying and she told me. Richard had told his mates what we had done on the Sunday. He said that it was really rubbish. Now he said he really hates me and everyone else seems to agree. I'm really sorry to let you down but it just happened. I really thought he loved me.

Love,

Penny'

'How can a boy be so cruel,' Penny's mother asked tearfully when I gave her back the letter. 'I suppose we could bring charges because they were both only fifteen. That's what her father wants to do, but I don't think that's a good idea. What do you think?'

'I don't think that the Police would do anything,' I said. 'They both agreed to what they did and they'll both be sixteen in a few months. I think that you should take Penny home for a few days and give her lots of love. We can say she's not well, which is certainly true.'

Penny went home and came back after the next weekend. Nothing more was said and the looks and whispers in the House died down. They both did well in their exams and Penny ended up doing Arts A levels before going on to read English at University. Looking back, I could not help wondering if she ever came across Shakespeare's 129th Sonnet in her studies. She would certainly know the truth of what he wrote:

> *Th'expense of spirit in a waste of shame*
> *Is lust in action; and till action, lust*
> *Is purjur'd, murd'rous, bloody, full of blame,*
> *Savage, extreme, rude, cruel, not to trust;*
> *Enjoy'd no sooner but despised straight;........*

At that time, in the 1990s, it was what a boy told his friends about the girl, and about what they had done which was spread around the school, to her great embarrassment. Now it is sexting, persuading either sex to send naked images on tablets and 'phones, all assumed to be in confidence but soon shared and shameful. The technology has changed but the bullying is still the same and the most recent survey suggests that four out of ten British teenage girls have been coerced into sexual activity which they did not want.

After Penny had left school, her mother came to see me and to thank me for the way in which we had helped her daughter. She knew that I was still involved in the College Health Ed. programme and suggested that I should use her daughter's experience to help other students. We agreed that this would help both girls and boys provided that all names and identifying details were changed. She even said that I should tell them about Penny's letter.

~

There was little we could do about sex which took place when boarders were at home or visiting friends but sex on the College site was strictly banned. But some of our students had no inhibitions at all. I was once on the morning train to Liverpool Street and hiding behind my copy of the Times when a senior officer in full uniform joined the carriage at Diss. When we had read enough of the Times, and looked at each other, he suddenly said:

'Good Morning, Mr Haden – we meet again! The last time I met you it was in your office and you were busy expelling my son from the College.'

I struggled to recognise him and then remembered. His son had indeed been expelled by me, right at the end of Year 11 for a major breach of the College Rules. On one of the last Sundays of term, after Chapel had finished, the Senior Housemaster on duty had marched the boy across from the Library, with his girl-friend behind him.

'I caught them at it,' said the Housemaster, pink faced and still clearly angry at the flagrant nature of the offence. 'There they were, just behind the Library, having sex on the Geography Department sand table. I have never seen such a shocking display! I'm handing them over to you, now!'

Was it the stupidity of two teenagers having sex in full view of everyone passing the Library, when there were acres of perfectly adequate woodland just next door, which so upset him? Or, perhaps, the sacrilege of using his Geography sand table for something so biological as their activity? I was not sure, but dealing with the matter was clearly my job. I warned them both that having sex in full view of staff and students was inevitably going to lead to an early end to their College careers. Both were in year 11 and had taken their GCSEs so what this meant was being sent home early and not coming back for the 6th Form. This they seemed to accept as reasonable. Perhaps the experience had been worth it.

Next morning, I met both sets of parents. Initially, they were angry at my proposed action but, under pressure from both the boy and the girl, calmed down and accepted the situation. As the girls said to her Mum:

the College has a rule which we all know and which has always been applied – if you're on the wrong side of the House, you're dead. We got a lot further, Mum, than being on the wrong side of the House – so I think we have to leave.

All of this I remembered while listening to the officer on the train from Norwich but I was quite unprepared for his next comment.

'I'm glad I've met you again because I want to thank you! That was the best thing the College ever did for my son – kicking him out, arrogant little twerp! We sent him to an all-boys school in the Thames valley as a 6th Form boarder and he did brilliantly. Passed all his A levels and even stroked the 1st VIII. Well done!'

He got up to leave the train at Manningtree and shook my hand.

'Look forward to meeting you again on the train some time.

18. Alcohol and Drugs

Lucy, the young liver and white cocker spaniel .....was the
most popular of the visiting drugs dogs.

Looking after other people's teenage children 24/7 is hard
enough without having them drunk or out of their heads on
drugs. If you have a 'family' of such children running into
the hundreds or even over a thousand, it becomes
impossible. Boarding schools can only operate with very
clear and enforced rules on consuming alcohol and taking
drugs and those who break such rules cannot be looked
after.

When I was a relatively junior boarder in our House
community, the rule was straightforward, no drinking and no
drugs – and if you were caught, you were out. There was one
evening near the end of the Christmas term when two of our
Prefects, celebrating their awards of Oxford places, brought
a bottle of vodka into the house and got roaring drunk. They
went home the next day and did not come back – not that
that worried them as they had their A levels, won their
Oxford places and had better things to do for the rest of the

school year. Alcohol could be a problem for boarding houses in the late 1950s but none of us knew much about drugs.

Alcohol was still a problem in the 1990s, and, I am sure, will always be. One particularly memorable occasion at Wymondham was the night of the 6th Form Formal Dinner, or rather the early hours of the following morning. Jenny and I were in the local version of Casualty, with two very drunk teenagers. The girl was still comatose. The boy woke up every half hour, to announce loudly,

'I'm shorry, Mr Haden, I'm shorry', before passing out again. Such are the joys of being '*in loco parentis*', and of taking our responsibilities very seriously. We got our two very miserable students back to the College Medical Centre later that day, both with splitting headaches and the need to explain to their parents why they were being sent home for a week with a final warning.

In the company of about three hundred 6th Form students and most of the staff, our two casualties had enjoyed a Christmas celebration evening in the last week of the term. The event was usually civilised and enjoyable for all, and had been held without major difficulty for many years. At the request of the organising committee, I always allowed the serving of a glass of weak Bucks Fizz before the meal and a glass of wine with it, to all who preferred this to fruit juice. But on that Christmas, the culture of heavy drinking by the young turned what had always been a pleasant evening, into a nightmare for the staff and a salutary lesson for many of the students.

In spite of clear warnings beforehand, and vigilance by the staff, several of the day students were already drunk by the time the meal started. The boys had spent the early evening 'pre-loading' at the local pub. Most of them were well under 18. More surprisingly, perhaps, several of the girls had been supplied with a bottle of wine each by their parents, while 'changing at a friend's home'. They were noisy, and one was sick, but this if disgusting, was not actually dangerous.

The boarders had greater difficulty in accessing alcohol. A handful persuaded friends to smuggle half bottles of vodka or rum into the boarding house, and then drank as much of it as they could as quickly as possible after the meal in preparation for the disco. The most badly effected girl was found unconscious, jammed into a cubicle of the girls' toilets. The boy had crept into bed and nearly choked when he was sick before passing out. Both were found by other students who had the good sense to get staff help and an ambulance as quickly as possible.

Schools, particularly boarding schools, accept responsibility for young people, and, quite rightly, can be held to account. One of my most harrowing duties as a Head had been attending the funeral of a 6th Former who had died when he choked in his own vomit at a friend's eighteenth birthday party. Every year after that, I told our 6th Formers about that funeral.

We had a very thorough programme of alcohol education through the taught curriculum and there is evidence that the desire by the young to 'get smashed out of their minds' is beginning to wane. As a national community, we are greatly troubled by the issue of drugs and young people. We need to be just as concerned about the widespread misuse of alcohol, and actually enforce the laws which control, in theory, its availability to the young.

Sadly, we live in a culture where heavy drinking by the young is accepted, often under the legal age limit, and even positively celebrated by the 'clubbing' and 'costa del alcohol' scene. Some boarding schools try to meet the demand for access to alcohol by having a bar in the school, where 6th form students can 'learn to drink sensibly'. I always resisted appeals for such a bar at Wymondham. Alcohol free schools make good sense, and are much easier to run.

~

But the misuse of drugs is also a huge issue for boarding schools. Even the most peaceful market town can host a well-developed drug supply network and any street-wise teenager knows how to get hold of the full range of drugs including the so-called 'legal highs'. Parents naively assume that schools can be kept free of such pressures but, sadly, however hard we try, there will be cases where violence and drug-related bullying creep into the school. Sometimes, parents are themselves the root of the problem.

John was in Year 7 when that year were still in the 11-16 houses, a slight boy with a sharp tongue and a very worldly-wise look. He seemed to find it hard to relate to his more childish contemporaries, preferring to make friends with older boys. The house staff noticed this but did not think it particularly odd. As his parents lived busy business lives through the week, they sent him to the school as a weekly boarder and tried to find time for John at home at the weekends. They did all that they could to support John and the school, taking part in our parents' functions and contributing generously to school fund raising.

'He seems happy enough,' his Mum commented on Sunday evening when she brought John back to the House and had a word with the House Tutor. 'But I just wish John told us a bit more about life at school.'

Towards the end of the term, the older boys in Y10 and Y11 seemed much less friendly towards John. One was caught hitting him, not hard but hard enough to hurt. John seemed strangely willing to accept these blows, but the staff clearly had to stop what looked like a clear case of bullying. Just talking to each of the older boys on their own proved ineffective, so the Head of House decided to see them together as a group.

'Why are you giving John such a hard time?' he asked them. None of them would say anything so they were all warned about the consequences of bullying and told that they were being watched closely.

One Thursday night in Prep, a vigilant House Tutor picked up a mysterious note. It had been dropped onto the floor just near to where John was sitting.

'Bring some good stuff in on Monday or you're dead. No more crap,' it said.

The Tutor continued to supervise Prep, and took the note to the Housemaster at the end of the evening.

'There's no clue as to who wrote it but it could have been intended for John or one of the other weekly boarders,' he told him.

That Sunday night, when John came back from his weekend, the Housemaster met him at the door and took him into the office.

'Just turn out your pockets for me, John,' he said quietly. 'Put everything on the desk.' John fished out a grubby handkerchief, some coins, a small penknife and a black lump with a very odd smell, a bit like Oxo.

'Why on earth are you bringing Oxo into school?' asked the astonished Housemaster. John burst into tears.

'They told me to, Sir,' he sniffed, but he would not say who 'they' were.

It was John's father who solved the mystery. He took the view that he had a right to smoke cannabis 'purely for recreational purposes' and kept a supply of cannabis resin in his desk at home. Over the term, he had noticed that the supply seemed to be running out rather more quickly than usual and he suspected that John had something to do with this. The boy denied it of course but the father made sure that no more resin was brought into the house.

John had been taking some of the cannabis resin each week and bringing it into school. He found a ready cash market for it amongst the Y11 boys who both befriended him and protected him. But when his supply began to dry up, he was too frightened to tell them and looked for an alternative. He started to cut his remaining supply of cannabis resin with increasingly large proportions of Oxo taken from his mother's kitchen. It looked similar to gullible teenagers but, as they said when the whole story finally came out 'it didn't work and it was crap for smoking!'

But what should a school do with a Y7 drug-dealer who had tried to cheat his customers? Fortunately for us and probably best for John, his parents decided that the time had come for the whole family to travel. As true children of the 1960s they took John and his sister with them on a long drive through the Middle East to India and beyond. That just left us with the Y11 customers to deal with, but by that time they were all off on 'exam leave' and had no intention of returning to the 6th Form.

~

Deputy Heads need to build a reputation for detective work if their role in boarding schools is to be really effective.

To be believed to have the talents of Inspector Morse and the ruthlessness of the Gestapo is half-way to cracking even the most well- planned breach of school rules.

One of our Deputies was an expert in the behaviour of teenagers but some cases were just too easy. 'Never underestimate the carelessness of the young', he would say after cracking what seemed a complete mystery to the rest of us on the staff. 'Take the case of the lost 'spliff'.'

The Y11 boarders had all gone downstairs one Sunday morning just before the exams in the summer term and made their way to the Leavers' Service in the Chapel. As usual, the matrons did a quick check of the empty dormitories to make sure that they were all suitably tidy. Parents sometimes brought their boarding children back on Sunday afternoons and carried their cases upstairs for them.

On this Sunday, the Matron found a fag-end on the dormitory floor. One of our boys had carelessly dropped the un-smoked half of his roll-up in his haste to get downstairs. In spite of all our efforts to convince boys that smoking was a bad idea and our rule that to be caught smoking in the boarding house was a very serious offence likely to end a promising school career, somebody was still smoking. As the fag-end was cold and could not be linked to any one of the six boys in that dormitory, the Matron sighed and decided to say nothing to the boys when they returned from Chapel. But she thought she should report it and left the evidence with a short explanatory note on the Deputy Head's desk.

Later that day, the Deputy Head summoned one of the Y11 boys to his office.

'This was found this morning on the floor of your dormitory, Michael,' he said. 'I know it's yours and I know what's in it.'

Michael was speechless for the first time in his life. When he got his voice back, he asked 'But how do you know it's mine, Sir? It could be anyone's.'

The Deputy Head carefully split the fag end to expose the rolled up card used to hold the contents in. 'I don't think so, Michael,' he said. 'Next time you roll a 'spliff', as I'm sure you will, don't use the end of your mother's business card.'

Michael was allowed to take his exams but he did not come back as a boarder. When the Matron heard how the Deputy Head had solved the crime, she said: 'We ask their mothers to make sure that all their clothes are labelled but I've never heard of personalised 'spliffs'.

~

Occasionally, I made bad mistakes. The Head of a independent day school 'phoned me one afternoon to ask if we had any boarding places in Y11. It is rare for a student to move school in the middle of a two year GCSE Course and I should have smelt a very large rat. But he was persuasive and had obviously promised to help the boys' parents to try to find him a boarding place as they 'were moving overseas in September and could not take him with them.' Apparently, they could not afford the cost of an independent boarding school place but could just about manage our boarding fees.

'He's very able and will get a string of A* grades even after the change,' the Head assured me. 'I'm sure he'll be an asset to your school.'

We invited the boy to an interview and met the mother as the father was said to be abroad. The senior Head of House who saw them asked some of his Y11 students to show the boy round the College while talking to the mother. Before they left us, he came to see me.

'I don't believe the story about the parents going abroad,' he told me. 'My boys think he's been kicked out of his school for dealing drugs. Don't touch him!'

I duly asked the mother to explain just why they wanted a boarding place for the boys and was told the same story again.

'We've got to go to Saudi,' she said. 'His Dad's new job is there and I can go but there's no provision for schooling.'

Unable to disprove what I had been told, and having a Y11 boarding bed to fill, I offered him a place with conditions. He came in September and for a month or two worked hard, did well and seemed settled with us. He stayed in the College when many of the Y11 boys went home for weekends and then said he was spending our Leave Weekend when everyone left the House, with his Grandmother in Norwich.

In fact, he went down to London, stayed with a friend and linked up with the group of young people who had been his suppliers for the drugs he had brought into his previous school. He came back into the House after the weekend and offered to supply one of our Y11 boarders. Unfortunately for him, his first potential customer was a member of our Peer Counselling group, who immediately reported the offer to his Head of House. He tried to deny the conversation but we trusted our Y11. The boy had to lose his boarding place with us as we had made our offer conditional on a term of impeccable behaviour.

~

In our efforts to ensure that the School was kept as free as possible from drugs, we worked closely with both the Police and the local Prison Service. Both used sniffer dogs to find drugs and they needed training opportunities for the dog to practice their skills in residential settings. Our school boarding houses provided just what they needed. We always discussed any visits from the Drugs dogs with the boarders in the House and made sure that they all knew what was happening. The aim was to give a clear message, 'if we want to catch you, we certainly can, but we would much rather you did not risk it.'

Lucy, the young liver and white cocker spaniel from the Prison Service, was the most popular of the visiting dogs. The boarders loved to make a fuss of her and to watch her searching the House for the samples which her handler hid in cupboards or under beds. Her favourite trick was to jump up onto a row of the metal lockers the boarders used for storing their books and games kit. She would run along the top, sniffing. When she suddenly stopped and got even more excited, the students knew that she had found the planted sample. If they were tempted to bring anything into the School, we just hoped that at least two days warning of the visit of the Prison drugs dog would ensure that they got rid of it in time. Colleagues claimed that the ducks on the pond could be seen swimming aimlessly round in circles on the day before the drugs dog came to visit.

With the agreement of the Sixth Form, we worked out a more sophisticated approach for their House. Respecting the privacy of each individual's room was important and we agreed that we would only allow the Police Alsatian to be trained in our Houses when the occupant of the room and a member of staff were both free to be there and witness the search. Again, we always made sure that the visit was well publicised so that any boarder who had anything to hide could get rid of it in good time.

In spite of all our efforts, sometimes students still got caught. One evening, the police team were training on a row of single rooms in the Upper Sixth area of the House during their evening study time. I escorted the Alsatian and handler from room to room, knocking on each in turn and checking beds, cupboards, lockers and bags as we went. One room had a planted sample which was found and the excited dog was rewarded.

We went to the next room and were welcomed by the occupant. The dog sniffed around the bed, the bags and the chest of drawers, and froze.

'Would you open that drawer, please?' said the policeman.

'No problem,' said the student, sliding the drawer open. The dog sniffed the folded clothes, and pushed its nose into the pocket of a pair of jeans.

'I think we do have a problem,' said the policeman. 'Could you just show us what the dog has found in that pocket?'

It was a small amount of 'skunk', the bit left over from a weekend away and completely forgotten. Not enough for the police to have to charge the student with possession, but enough for a very serious warning and a requirement from the School for the boarder to have to take his exams as a day student.

On another occasion, the sniffer dogs really did find something to get excited about. We were hosting a broadcast of the BBC's 'Question Time' in the College library and using the Sports Hall as a base for the technicians to shelter in from the March wind and rain. Because one of the politicians on the Panel had been Secretary of State for Northern Ireland and was still reckoned to be an IRA target, the whole area had to be searched for explosives. The dogs checked every building and came to a locked store-room door. Both Labradors became very excited. The PE staff were asked to find the store-room door key, which they did. The two dogs shot into the dark room and came out wagging their tales with wrapping paper in their triumphant teeth. The police handler looked puzzled. Why was birthday present paper so exciting to the dogs?

The Head of Girls' PE giggled. 'Clever dogs, they found the remains of my birthday cake. They must have smelt the marzipan.'

With nothing more explosive than a few scraps of cake, 'Question Time' could be recorded.

~

All our houses had effective fire alarm systems which were directly connected to the local Fire Brigade Headquarters to ensure that any fire problem could be dealt with within minutes. As a result, the Governors and staff agreed that the whole College campus would be a no-smoking area, within all buildings and anywhere on site. This did not of course prevent habitual smokers from walking into the woods and lighting up well away from the buildings but it did ensure that false alarms from cigarette smoke were comparatively rare. Occasionally, we forgot to warm visitors of this blanket prohibition, with entertaining results.

One Sunday morning, just before the start of the College Chapel service, two very excited twelve year-olds demanded to see me, urgently.

'We caught him, Sir. He lit up behind the Chapel and was puffing away in all his church kit. We thought you should know because it's against our rules, isn't it, Sir!'

Trying to keep a straight face, I thanked them for their vigilance and assured them that I would have a word with our clerical visitor. He was a very distinguished Bishop. I did have a word with him after the morning serviced to thank him for his sermon and to explain our no-smoking rule just in case he felt the need to light up again before he left us. He was very apologetic and thanked me profusely for saving him from being subjected to a citizens' arrest by two small boys.

19. In Sickness and in Health

Working alongside the teaching staff at Wymondham were the Matrons, in teams of three per house, eighteen in all. Their flats were on the top floors and again these formed the barriers between the boys' sides and the girls' sides. Some of the women who took on these critically important roles were single but many were happily married ladies. They were prepared to take on sleeping–in duties for two nights a week and every third weekend in term-time to relieve the permanent members of the house matron team. Some were former nurses who preferred working with fit and healthy young men and young women and providing them with pastoral care and support outside teaching hours. Others had experience of working in residential care for young people.

The role also involved what could be described as 'general housekeeping', such as organising the laundry, and supervising boarders' use of the house washing machines and ironing room as our boarders did all their own personal laundry. We even ran a very popular annual inter-house 'boarding skills' competition between teams of Y8 boarders. This included washing a sheet in a House machine, ironing a school shirt, making a bed including changing the cover on a duvet and cleaning a pair of shoes – their own of course! Their mothers thought that this was a wonderful idea!

Our matrons also ensured that the teams of cleaners who worked in the houses did a good job and were properly respected by the boarders. If one of the boarders needed a paracetamol or a plaster, they went to the matron on duty and usually got a chat and sometimes a cup of tea as well. When we had staff crises, such as a 'flu epidemic and one or more houses ran out of staff to 'sleep in' in the Matron's duty rooms, senior staff helped by taking an overnight bag with them across to the house and covering the duty. We always tried to do this on a gender specific basis, women covering for matrons and either women or men covering for female or male house tutors because we did not wish to compromise our gender specific staffing patterns.

For some matrons, the provision of a home and meals while on duty was some compensation for the relatively low salaries although these were competitive against other care-staff roles. The job demanded energy and maturity and a genuine interest in working with teenagers in all their rich variety. Above all, matrons had to work well together in a team and in many ways embodied this key outcome for all our boarders. They very often had to carry the confidences of the boarders, especially the girls and being calm, discrete and un-shockable was part of their brief. Matrons saw themselves as 'surrogate mums' and very much enjoyed this role, being acknowledged as a very important part of the College team.

~

When we were visited by the party of staff and students from Arua who came from the school which Jenny and I had taught at many years before, their Ugandan Head took back to his school many ideas about how to improve their boarding arrangements. He had become convinced that their tradition of having members of staff responsible for boarding houses but not actually living with the boarders was no longer acceptable. Leaving supervision to senior boys and senior girls in the role of prefects, following the traditional practice of English Public schools, had to go. He ensured that any new boarding houses in his school were built with staff flats adjacent to the dormitories. His school could not afford resident matrons so he re-designated the lady teachers who looked after the girls as 'matrons' and the male teachers who looked after the boys became 'patrons'. We could not fault either his logic or his knowledge of the Latin roots of English!

~

Most of our boarders were very fit young people but just occasionally we were asked to admit a chronically sick child, usually the younger sibling of a boarder. Stephen came for interview at 11 with his parents, teachers from a town in North Norfolk. As his mother explained, Stephen had cystic fibrosis which was at that time a life threatening condition which took many children before they reached their twenties. We already had his very fit sister in our school, were we prepared to care for Stephen? We consulted Chris and his Matrons. Could they look after him?

Stephen thrived at the College. He had daily sessions of vigorous physiotherapy from the Matrons – as Chris said, he was the only boarder we were allowed to hit, hard on his back to help him to cough up the phlegm which threatened to drown him. He came close to the edge several times when a heavy cold could have turned into pneumonia, but he survived. Thanks to the matrons, he took part in all that the College could offer him, left with good A levels and got a good degree.

~

Our College origins in the huts of a WWII US Army Air Force Hospital provided us with our Sick Bay, occupying the two huts which during the War had housed the operating theatres. They were right at the end of the rows of huts which formed the wards with a concrete overhead gantry carrying massive heating pipes to each of the huts. Our two

243

nursing Sisters provided twenty four hour cover for any sick students and helped the College Doctor to run daily surgeries there for students and staff. Sometimes, their efforts were life-saving.

On the last day of the Christmas term 1995, I took the final College Assembly in the Sports Hall, wished the College a very Happy Christmas and walked back across the College to my Office. Halfway there, I met my Secretary running towards me. She never ran. Clutched in her hand was a scrap of paper. 'Boy very ill – come NOW, Sick Bay.' I ran. The Sister on Duty was sitting by the side of a bed. Lying still and silent was the wraith like body of a teenager who only twenty four hours before I had seen score the winning try in the last U15 Rugby match of the term. He hardly seemed to be breathing and was an ashen white with just a hint of pink rash on his cheek. The time was 1.50 pm.

'Richard came across this morning from his house,' the Sister said, 'feeling a bit under the weather but he saw the Doc this morning at half past ten. By 12, he was beginning to complain about the bright light in here and he was sick. He went very pale and I realised that he was very poorly so I called the doctor back. By 1 o'clock he was here and we both agreed that Richard was going down fast – then the rash started to appear. I knew what it was because I had a case at the N and N (our Norwich Hospital). The Doc had some penicillin in his bag so we started giving it even before calling the ambulance.'

Richard was rushed into the N and N Hospital with our Sister in the ambulance holding a drip with more penicillin. By 2.15 pm his mother had arrived at the College having been told by the Office that her son was very ill. He was admitted at 2.30 pm in a critical condition. By 3.30pm the consultant had 'phoned me to say that we were 'to fear the worst'. By 7 pm, he was on a ventilator in intensive care. At that point in the evening, I had to go to a party for staff leaving that term. I 'phoned Richard's parents at the Hospital and they told me how poorly he was.

Then the Norfolk Public Health Doctor 'phoned me to advise me that one of my students had been diagnosed with Meningitis B, which by then I had known for some hours. I asked her whether we should let other parents know that a boarder had been diagnosed with meningitis so that they could watch their children very carefully.

The Doctor said: 'No – please don't. We are not yet ready to go public because we're not ready to deal with the inevitable flood of enquiries – please leave it until Saturday morning.'

That conversation began a five-day conflict of understanding. I explained that our day students came from all over East Anglia and our boarders from all over the world. Many would by now be on their way to international flights and could well develop symptoms before they reached home. They were at risk and their parents had to be warned to be vigilant. She had no experience of boarding schools and had only the interests of her County medical system to protect. She was adamant – no information until Saturday morning, and then we should notify '*all known contacts from the previous 48 hours*'. We should advise any close contacts that they should see their doctors for preventative antibiotic treatment as soon as possible.

When I asked her what '*close contact*' meant, she said that the usual advice was those in '*kissing contact*'.

She had never dealt with a case of meningitis in a boarding school before. It had been diagnosed on the last day of term. The boy now fighting for his life in hospital had been running around the College for the past week. He had been in lessons in most departments. He had visited most of the boarding houses and had taken a full and active part in the House disco on the previous evening. That happy event had been enjoyed by one hundred and eighty teenagers, boys and girls making full use of several bunches of mistletoe. We had to assume that all the members of his house had been in '*kissing contact*' and all the other students of the College had been potential contacts over the previous 48 hours.

In the days before emails and text-messages, we had no choice but to prepare letters advising all parents and carers of the case of meningitis and then send them out by post. They would reach all East Anglia addresses by Monday morning. By that time, some of our students might be dead.

Then Pubic Health asked for further delays '*because it was now the weekend and we do not have the staff*', but I knew on Saturday afternoon that we could wait no longer. There were hundreds of families, scattered across almost every Continent, who needed to know that their children were at risk. By mid-night on the Saturday we had phoned them all, world-wide. By the Sunday morning, Richard was still alive.

A GP in Thetford had sent one of our boys into West Norfolk Hospital with suspected meningitis on Tuesday but did not hear from Norfolk Public Health until Thursday. By that time, the Norfolk Public Health Doctor had '*gone on leave*' under the strain and another was '*in charge of our outbreak*'. Richard was still alive.

There is a vaccine for some types of Meningococcal Meningitis and the decision was taken to offer it to the students who had been in contact with our two cases and to their parents.

'What do you mean by '*contact*'?' I stupidly asked again.

'Kissing contact', back came the reply, again. We sent out yet another set of letters to all parents of College students and all guardians advising vaccination.

By the Thursday morning of the first week of the Christmas holiday, Richard was beginning to show signs of improvement. The boy in the West Norfolk was much better and a third possible case turned out to be food poisoning. We had turned the corner. By Friday, a week after the College had closed for Christmas, no further local cases had been reported and we heard of none from abroad. We could begin to enjoy the holiday.

The barrage of 'phone calls which the Office had handled magnificently was easing off and what had been a disaster story in the eyes of the local media, TV, radio, papers and grapevine, could be re-presented as a 'good news' story. Thanks to the prompt action and professional skill of our Sick Bay Sister, no-one had died. We had helped the Local Public Health administration to understand a boarding school. But no-one was much interested in Good News.

~

Sadly, we did have another case of meningitis two years later, although it occurred in the middle of the summer holiday and there was no established link with the first cases. One of our day students was camping with his family on the Isle of White when he told them he was going to bed early because he did not feel well. They thought that he had a '*bit too much sun*' and suggested he sleep it off in his tent. They found him dead in the morning. When we all came back to College in September, we held a memorial service for him which all his friends and the staff could go to. That brought it home to us all just how frail life is and just how vigilant you have to be with meningitis.

~

Two years later, meningitis struck the College yet again. By cruel coincidence, a boy in the same house as Richard had gone home for the weekend and become unwell. His parents, fully aware from the information provided four years before of the dangers of meningitis had themselves taken him into hospital and he was kept in overnight for observation. In the morning, meningococcal meningitis was confirmed but he was responding well to antibiotic treatment and was in no danger. How was it possible for a community all of whom had received meningitis immunisation four years before to have yet another case – and in the same house?

'That was B', I was told. 'This is C.'

We followed the medical advice to provide all students in that house, boarding and day, and all house staff with a preventative course of antibiotics just in case any of them had become infected. I decided to include myself to show solidarity and so became aware of the interest that the boarders were showing in the colour of their urine. At the time, a well-known mobile phone company had a particularly catchy TV advert. '*The future's bright, the future's orange!*' became the House mantra for the rest of the term.

~

Our life-saving 'Sick Bay' eventually had to be replaced as the corrugated iron of the huts fell to bits. The ground floors of two staff houses became vacant and the garages between them were adapted to form a new Medical Centre with small wards for boys and for girls. The first floors of both houses formed flats for the nursing staff. We created an attractive and effective medical unit at minimal capital cost.

It still serves those of over six hundred boarders who need treatment out of their boarding Houses.

~

I doubt if I am the only boarding school Head who has been accused of being '*married to the school*'. Such is the total immersion of leading a boarding community of up to a thousand young people and staff, that other relationships can seem secondary, including that of partner or parent. It should not be so and many have worked hard to ensure that the needs of spouses and families are recognised.

It is partly the fact that there is no escape from the pressure of events during term-time. For one half of the relationship, there is an unrelenting demand for time, for discussion, for decisions, for advice. Governors, parents, colleagues, students, officers of public bodies both local and national, all assume a right of access and an attentive ear. It can seem that the world is the school. I well remember driving off the College campus in the midst on one of our major crises and discovering that life in the local town was going on as normal, people were still shopping, dogs were going for walks, the Banks were still there.

For one's spouse, especially if he or she does not have a job and a life outside the school, it can be very lonely to be at the centre of all this activity and yet still an observer. Staff do not easily relate to 'the Head's wife' or 'the Head's husband'. There is no easy access to the social hubs, the Staff Room, the School Office. Working in the school is made much more difficult when one had to face the pressures of difficult classes and awkward colleagues, conscious that any sign of weakness is bound to be discussed in less than sympathetic terms.

For the Head's children, it can be even more difficult. Our son chose to stay in Lincolnshire as a boarder with his friends rather than come to Norfolk with his parents. We both thought he was right, but we both missed having him at home. There are some schools, and King Edward VI in Louth was one of them, where the civilised atmosphere and focus on learning rather than surviving makes it possible for all the teenage children of the staff who want to come to the school can happily do so. We benefitted from that as a family, with all four of us, two sons as students, mother as teacher and father as head, enjoying a parallel but different experience of school. It would not have been as easy at Northallerton or in Norfolk as both were bigger schools with rougher edges.

In the boarding houses, life for married couples was tough as well. Yet it was their resilience and their capacity to cope which made the idea of looking after over a hundred boarders even possible. Over all the years we spent working in the largest State boarding school in Western Europe, there was no marriage in a boarding house that broke down. Some came very near to the edge. Some may have become partially detached. But none actually broke. For the young people who were in those Houses, that example of the surviving strength of a relationship was hugely important. We used to joke about the College ethos of '*triumph over adversity*', the ethos which was celebrated in the College song:

> '*Let Wymondham College students see*
> *That they fulfil their destiny,*
> *In triumph, in adversity, ...Floreat Sapientia!*'

When Sir Lincoln Ralphs wrote those words, and the College went on to become as successful as it is today, I wonder whether enough credit is and will continue to be given to those whose strong personal relationships which turned a school into a community and held the place together, especially at times of real challenge.

~

After eight years at the College, my own health began to show signs of strain. It was not that I was suffering from any specific life-threatening disease, just that the warnings were becoming clear that working at this level of stress was not a good long-term way of earning a living. At that time, the Department for Education had offered funds to Local Authorities for early retirement for Heads on the grounds of long service and increased stress. In Norfolk, the Secondary Heads met to discuss what we christened the *'clapped out heads special offer'*. Three of us decided to apply. Although the College was a Foundation School, the County still offered pension advice and personnel management support to schools.

The response from County Hall was short and discouraging. Effectively, we were told that we were far too expensive to be given early retirement with pension enhancement. The County personnel expert just laughed.

'We cannot afford your level of cost,' he said. 'This scheme is to help long-serving heads of small primary schools – not expensive secondary Heads, however clapped out they might be, and any way, you're not yet clapped out!'

So after eight years in Norfolk and eighteen years as a Head, I resigned and found another job.

20. A Vision for State Boarding ?

Lord Nash challenged us at the SBSA Conference in November 2014 to articulate our vision for State Boarding schools, to explain more clearly why State Boarding schools were important and could offer something very valuable to disadvantaged children. Some of us at that conference would prefer a vision which focused on a return to grammar schools. I don't share their vision. Why would one adopt a system which would exclude three quarters of one's potential applications for boarding places, including girls like Anna? There are even those nationally who would advocate a return to the use of corporal punishment to solve the problem of indiscipline in England's state schools. Few of us who work in schools would agree to wield the cane again – I would not.

Some of the Heads meeting at Holyport College said that they wanted a clear national Government policy on boarding in State schools, just as the French were beginning to develop under Nicholas Sarkozy. Having worked under Idi Amin's Government which created terror, I do not share this interest in over-riding national policies. I prefer the British talent for developing pragmatic solutions to local challenges even if this undermines a national system and creates a mixed economy of schools.

But we should be able to help very many more children who would benefit from an assisted boarding place and there should be a State Boarding opportunity open to every family across the UK. That would require national planning to preserve and enhance the network of SBSA schools to ensure that there was one within an hour's drive of all areas of England.

Currently there are significant areas of England which do no have this near access to State Boarding opportunities,

The current distribution of SBSA schools, showing

selective schools as ● and comprehensive schools as o

State Boarding has survived but there were still only 5,000 places. Some slow growth had started but we needed much more. There should be significant expansion of provision. Ray McGovern, Head of St George's School, Harpenden, and another former Chair of both SBSA and BSA, has proposed an initial expansion to 10,000 places.

This could include expanding the current boarding houses and building new ones, as we have done over the past five years. There are areas of the country where there is no comprehensive State Boarding opportunity within an hour's drive of every home. It would be good if the expansion of places could also ensure a better national spread. If that can be achieved by Government support for State Boarding, there is a case for letting Heads and Governors get on with the job of running their schools with the minimum of control from the centre.

Some of us at Holyport that November felt that it was demeaning to State school Heads to be told that the solution to our problems lay in encouraging Heads and Governors of famous Independent schools to take over the leadership of the worst performing state schools in order to improve them. 'What can they teach us?', was the feeling, as we were entertained by Eton in their magnificent Tudor Dining Hall? I have no difficulty about schools harnessing talent from either side of the State/Independent divide if it produces better schools and more opportunities for the pupils we serve. State school Heads move into the Independent sector and vice versa. Matrons from Wymondham can become Dames at Eton, and vice versa. We need to find talent and leadership from all sources if schools are to improve.

~

When the senior staff of Wymondham College went away together to the local 'spa hotel' with a team of Governors, we hoped to 'build the team'; that was the justification for the expense. But what we were really doing was to try to work out what the College was for – what we hoped pupils would gain from up to seven years in our care. We were thinking mainly of the boarders as they were the

254

pupils for whom the College was founded and around whom the College was organised, those who formed a community as well as a school.

After various bonding exercises, which seemed to involve odd tasks like throwing and catching eggs to build trust, a messy business, we sat down to work out a 'Mission Statement', our vision for the College. Later that evening, we took it back to our colleagues still doing Prep Duty and asked what they thought. There was some initial scepticism – after all they had not had the away-day or the chance to throw an egg at the Principal and the Chair of Governors - but gradually, the wording gained support. It went though some mutations, but ended up as:

Wymondham College exists to encourage young people to develop into good citizens, to aim for excellence in all that they attempt, to communicate effectively, work well in teams and to enjoy life.'

This vision of what the College was all about survived for a number of years as the agreed Mission Statement. More recently, it has developed into something slightly different: *to enable young people to become happy, successful and useful citizens, to aim for excellence in all they do and to find fulfilment in life.* It is interesting that at a time when so many schools have said that they are about *'excellence for all'*, the College has remained true to the more realistic aspiration of *'aiming for excellence'*.

With the expansion of day and day boarding places at the College, it has grown to a current total 11-18 roll of 1340 including 633 boarders. There will always be a tension between the needs of boarders and those of day pupils as so many parents living in the area will want to get their sons and daughters into a school which has such a wealth of opportunities. This is primarily because it is organised as a boarding school. One result is that Heads and Governors of popular SBSA schools spend a lot of time and effort on recruiting boarders while having to restrict day access through admission policies which used to depend on catchment areas but now rely on proximity.

Since the Education Reform Act 1988, parents have been able to express a choice of school for their children. This change combined with the funding of schools on the basis of the age and number of pupils has created a competitive market for schools to operate in. Parental choice, always at the heart of the way in which the independent sector operated, became, for the first time, a reality for state schools.

For the handful of State Boarding schools that operated not as day schools with a boarding house but as majority or high proportion boarding schools, this move to parental choice may not have been much of a change. Schools like Old Swinford Hospital, Cranbrook, Sexey's and Wymondham College had always recruited their boarding applicants mainly by parental choice. Parents had to choose a boarding place or be supported in that choice by a funding authority. Such schools only use proximity for their minority of day places and the switch to proximity has had a dramatic effect on house prices in the areas near popular schools. That has been true of schools like Wymondham College which offer day places while remaining organised as boarding schools. It will no doubt be true for Academies like Holyport College as their local day reputation grows. For boarding places, proximity has never been relevant as for such places, what ensures that the school has a future is the quality of what it is able to offer. State Boarding schools provide a service to parents and their children in an open and very competitive market – they have to be sensitive to parental choice and parental confidence in a way shared by no other group of state schools.

The real challenge for the Heads of such State Boarding schools is that parents may have such differing views of how the school should meet their demands. Mrs H-J, mother of the owner of the pink furry pencil case, clearly thought that her daughters' immediate needs, day or night, should take priority over my reasonable interest in a good night's sleep. Few other parents ever made such demands but some have tried.

~

Perhaps the final words in this account of State Boarding should come from the boarders themselves. There are three particularly memorable comments made to me by boarders about the challenges of leading boarding schools.

The first was within a few months of arriving in Norfolk. On my way over to the Sports Hall for the College Assembly on a Saturday morning, as the staff and students were walking across the campus from their lessons and their Houses, one of the Y9 boarders walked alongside me.

'Excuse me, Sir,' he said politely. 'May I say something to you?'

'Of course,' I said, 'provided that it's not rude!'

'Oh no, Sir,' he said. It's just that I've noticed. You do come out a lot.'

I knew what he meant as the Staff had by then discovered the same thing, although they were perhaps not so keen to have me turn up unexpectedly in their distant Nissen Huts. Secondary Heads at that time were being encouraged to develop a collaborative model of leadership, a model which I had struggled with, preferring to be very much 'hands on'. The problem with collaboration as I saw it was that it took a lot of time discussing what the Senior Leadership Team eventually agreed should be done.

My preference was to delegate key areas of responsibility to senior colleagues and then to leave them to take the decisions that needed to be made, accepting full responsibility for implementing them. I found that I could trust the Vice Principals and the Heads of House to run their own areas of the College and very seldom had to become directly involved. That did not mean that I was not highly visible around the College – if anything I was much too visible for some boarders!

For every week in term-time, the three Senior Staff and I agreed to cover one period of 24 hours, starting and ending at midday, Monday/Tuesday, Tuesday/Wednesday, Wednesday /Thursday, Thursday/Friday.

We each then had one full weekend Friday/Monday on call, twice each term. When through staff sickness or other commitments we were struggling to cover all boarding over-night duties, this team of Senior staff would turn up with an overnight bag to 'sleep in' in a Tutor's flat or even as a Matron. This ensured that the College always maintained the separation of girls and boys in the Houses. I or one of the Vice-Principals would always be spotted on our way into a boarding house to do these cover duties and the Head of House would breathe a sigh of relief knowing that it was likely to be a very peaceful night. The 'heavy mob' were around!

The other duty which these cover arrangements sometimes included was to support the Sick Bay staff in dealing with any emergencies. Saturday afternoons could be especially busy in the winter terms when there could be up to six Rugby and Hockey matches on the College fields. Just occasionally, pupils would be injured. If it was serious, an ambulance would be called. Usually one of the Sick Bay sisters would go with the casualty in the ambulance to the Hospital. If another accident then occurred, one of the senior staff would either go with the casualty in another ambulance or take him or her to Accident and Emergency by car.

I was on call one November weekend when a visiting Rugby player broke a leg badly and had to be taken to hospital with our Sister in an ambulance. It was just a few moments later when a large teenager playing Rugby for our 3rd XV suffered a bad cut to his knee. There was no broken bone, just a lot of blood and a lot of moaning – Max was not one to be brave in the face of injury. We got the bleeding to stop by pressing hard on the cut and he was loaded into the back of my car, well wrapped in towels to ensure no blood leaked onto the seat.

Some hours later, he had been stitched up by a young doctor in A and E who was not at all impressed by Max's wailing even when given a painkilling injection in his leg. I drove Max back to College. He was the son of an indulgent mother who had separated from her husband. Max spent every summer with her, being given so much food that he returned to College every year in September very over-weight. By Christmas, he was fairly fit, having enjoyed playing a lot of enthusiastic rugby, not very skilfully. On our way back to the College, I asked him about being a boarder.

'I found it very difficult at first,' he said. 'I was very home-sick and no-one seemed to care much about me, but eventually I found some good friends.'

'What,' I asked Max, 'is the best thing about being a boarder?'

He thought for a long time, nursing his sore knee. 'I think it is that you're always there,' he said.

He did not mean me – we had hardly spoken that year as he had not yet been in my Health Ed. classes.

'What I mean is that, no matter what the time of day or even night, at the College, there's always someone I can go to and share my problems with. It's not like that at home. Dad's never there and Mum spends a lot of time with her friends. But at the College, there's always someone there.'

A Head 'who came out a lot' was noticed by one boarder and adults who were 'always there' were valued by another boarder. The third comment came just as I was leaving the College. The Governors had a collection for me and presented me with the original drawing of the curved Mrs Tablock and her colleague who were the wrong shape for normal classrooms. The staff clubbed together and bought Jenny and me a very fine garden bench, a comfortable oak seat on which to while away a long and, they hoped, happy retirement. We still have both gifts and they remind us of many happy moments at the College.

On my bookcase at home I have another gift. It is a small statue of a wise owl in a mortar board clutching a book. It had been bought by Anna, one of those six girls in the Peel A dormitory. When she was 16 in Y11 and about to leave herself to go to Catering College, she had bought the owl out of her pocket money. She wanted me to have it because I had done something for her. I had offered her Grandmother a boarding place for her at Wymondham College, a place supported by a County boarding grant. Granny had brought her up as best she could but was no longer able to look after her except for short holiday periods. Becoming a boarder had given Anna a new life.

'No-one had ever said to me that I was good at anything until I came here,' she said. 'Even after I came, I was still pretty rubbish at most things. But you said I was very good at something very important – do you remember?'

I did. She had been a member of that six-bed dormitory of particularly ambitious girls. Two turned out to be very good at games, one was a gifted musician and two were very good at their school work. These five spent a lot of time falling out, arguing and behaving like typical teenagers. Anna had not seemed to be good at anything, but she was. When she had settled in and was proudly wearing the same smart school uniform as everyone else, Anna was the one who got them to work together when there was a need to clear things up. She was the one who comforted the miserable one when her father in the Army Air Corps had to go to Kosovo with NATO. She was the one who solved the problem of the shame of 'nits'.

One of the girls in her A dorm had lost her Mum though cancer over the summer holiday. As if that wasn't bad enough, her distraught father was then told by a well-meaning Aunt that the girl also had head-lice. It was just before the start of the September term. There was no time to deal with this so the embarrassed father had to tell the Matron about the problem on taking the girl to the House. He was assured that only people with clean hair got nits and that Matrons were experts in dealing with them.

Anna found the girl in floods of tears in the dormitory and put her arm around her shoulders to comfort her. The girl pulled away and said, 'don't come near me. I've got nits!' Anna thought for a moment and said, 'I've got them too.' By the time the girls got back from boarders' tea to finish unpacking their bags, Anna had persuaded all six in the dormitory that they had nits. They all reported to Matron and all sat around with anti-nit foam in their hair, being treated for nits together. Thirteen year olds can provide a community of human warmth and support when given the opportunity. Sometimes they can do a better job of caring that the adult professionals sent in to counsel those in need.

Anna was also the one who stayed awake all night with the girl who was to play the flute for the House in the Mair Cup, had a panic attack and said she could not play. She was the one who had eventually flourished at the College, discovering that by hard work she could get five good GCSE grades and go on to a Catering Course at College. She was very good at persuading others that they could get on with each other and I had told her so. She now manages a successful hotel and has her own family, and I still have her Wise Owl statue sitting on my bookshelf. She is a fine example of Edward Thring of Uppingham's belief that *'every child can do something well'*. He never forgot his experience as a Curate in Gloucester teaching in the parish elementary school, experience which convinced him that "*to teach the slow and ignorant with success is the only test of proficiency and intellectual power.*" So much for the modern focus on League Tables and Oxbridge places.

~

Those of us who are committed to boarding schools have to recognise that boarding is not for every child. Most will be better looked after by their own loving parents. But some pupils need boarding opportunities if they are to thrive and the nation's State Boarding schools can provide those opportunities. These are schools which are good enough for caring and informed parents to choose for their own sons and daughters. They will have a stable core of 'choice' boarders and be strong enough to offer perhaps one in five or six places to 'needs' boarders. Children offered such places will flourish in the care of such schools, as Lords Adonis and Nash both flourished thanks to their experience as boarders.

These schools should be led by Heads who 'come out a lot' and are not afraid of their own visibility. Such schools are served by committed staff who can create stable and successful House communities. They should be supported by Governors who know how to be 'critical friends'. These are the good State Boarding schools which can then offer children the opportunity to thrive.

All the indications are that this vision for State Boarding will continue to develop over the next twenty years. Both major parties are now interested in the future of such schools as a stable and valuable national resource. Now that we have majority Conservative government for up to five years, there is the opportunity to continue the development of a State Boarding system. My hope is that those who serve the pupils of State Boarding Schools for the next fifty years will find as much professional and personal satisfaction as my fifty years in State Boarding has given me.

John Haden
Oakham, 2015

Notes and References

Preface

- The global popularity of J K Rowling's *'Harry Potter'* books has provided recent generations of children, especially boys, with a knowledge of boarding schools, at least of the mythical 'Hogwarts' variety. Enid Blyton's *'Mallory Towers'* books provided girls of earlier generations with a picture of life at a fictional girls' boarding school. There has been very little published about boarding schools in the UK State sector since Royston Lambert's *'The State and Boarding Education'* Methuen 1966.

- John Rae when Head of Westminster School published *'Letters from School'* Fontana/Collins 1987, *'Delusions of Grandeur'* Harper Collins 1993 and *'The Old Boys' Network'* Short Books 2009. These provided the best accounts of what it was like to lead one of England's great independent boarding schools. His wife, Daphne Rae, published her own account *'A World Apart'* Lutterworth Press 1983 of her experience of life at Harrow, Taunton and Westminster, which ruffled a few feathers.

- More recently, Heads have been reticent about writing about their own schools. The most distinguished current Head who is also a published author, is Sir Anthony Seldon, retired Master of Wellington College. He has published over thirty books, including many distinguished political biographies and has written widely about the cultivation of mindfulness in schools. Seldon has also written very many articles about the independent/state divide and the need to move away from what he calls 'factory schools'.

- Tony Little has very recently published his thoughts on education, having led three independent boarding schools, most notably Eton College. *'An Intelligent Person's Guide to Education'* Bloomsbury 2015 sets out, among other things, a wealth of good advice for parents, an English teacher's plea for the importance of developing a love of reading and his belief in the transformative effect of good, modern boarding schools, independent and state.

- Dominic Carman in his *'Heads Up: the challenges facing England's leading head teachers'* Thistle 2013) quotes from a number of Independent school Heads but from none of their State school colleagues.

- There are a number of guides to public schools such as *'Cradles of Success: Britain's Premier Public Schools'* by Mario Di Monaco University of Buckingham Press 2012. Victoria Davies Jones and Jennifer Ma *'Boarding Schools: All You Need To Know'* John Catt Educational 2014 gives good advice to parents looking for a boarding school for their children and lists many sources of information, but it does not refer to the State Boarding Schools Association or any single UK State Boarding school.

- Dame Sally Coates' *'Head Strong, 11 lessons of school leadership'* John Catt Educational 2015 is an account of how she led Burlington Danes out of Special Measures to become an Academy with outstanding judgments in every Ofsted Category – very much an inspiring 'how to do it' book.

Chapter 1 Why Boarding and why state?

- For the history of King's School Canterbury and of Ripon Grammar School, see the school websites; information about developments at Ripon from a conversation with Martin Pearman, Headmaster, in January 2015

- Information on the CEA from the Ministry of Defence and from a conversation with Robert Moorhouse, Bursar, Wymondham College March 2015

- See written evidence submitted to the Parliamentary Defence Committee by the Director of the Boarding Schools Association on *The Armed Forces Covenant in Action? Part 3: Educating the children of Service personnel'* February 2013

- Rowena Mason's article in *The Guardian* 17 February 2015 sets out David Cameron's change of view

- Matthew Holehouse and Gordon Rayner in *The Telegraph* 29 Jun 2014 quote David Blunkett on Prince Charles' views

- *'Access to Grammar schools for disadvantaged pupils'*: A report of interviews with Grammar and Primary Head teachers by Amy Skipp and Fay Sadro The Sutton Trust November 2013

- Information on fees from Sexey's School website

- See Graeme Paton in *The Telegraph* 2nd June 2014 on *All private schools to be given 'Ofsted-style inspections'*

- Information from: *'State of the Nation 2014: Social Mobility and Child Poverty in Great Britain'* Cabinet Office, Department for Education and Department for Work and Pensions 20 October 2014

- For reports on the educational background of leading social groups, see http://www.suttontrust.com/about-us/us/social-mobility/ and Sutton Trust reports '.....*leading scientists and scholars*' 2009, '.....*UK's top solicitors, barristers and judges*' 2010

- The NFER has published a very useful summary of *'Boarding schools in Europe: a role in publicly-funded provision?'* which includes information on Sarkozy's scheme and *'Internats d'excellence (boarding schools of excellence): lessons from Sourdun'* January 2014

Chapter 2 Schools for people like us

- For an interesting contemporary equivalent to the loss of my yellow cap, see the advice to parents of St Paul's School boys who cross Hammersmith Bridge: 'tell them to take off their blazers and wear a hoodies to avoid having their mobile 'phones stolen on their way home' – *The Times* 1st December 2014

- Information on Ridley Hall from Haydon Bridge High School web site

Chapter 3 Boarding Need

- Royston Lambert *'The State and Boarding Education'* 1966 has a full discussion of boarding need as interpreted by Local Authorities

- % of children living with both parents is now rising again, +3% in two years, according to the family stability indicator study by the Department of Work and Pensions, March 2015

- *'Boarding Provision for Vulnerable Children – Pathfinder'* report by Department for Schools, Children and Families April 2007

Chapter 4 Boarding Houses

- For the details of State Schools with boarding houses, see the SBSA website 'Find a school' pages
- Figures for schools over the last fifty years taken from:
  - Appendix 4 of Royston Lambert *'The State and Boarding Education'* 1966
  - Hansard HC Deb 31 January 1992 vol 202 cc717-9W
  - Current SBSA website data
- De Aston School website and conversation with Stephen Bunney, Head of Boarding, May 2015
- Skegness Grammar School website and conversation with John and Helen Nuttall, Boarding Houseparents, May 2015
- Thomas Adam School website
- QE Academy Trust website and conversation with Muriel Grimes, Head of Boarding and Lee Smith, Deputy Head of Boarding, November 2014
- Ridley Hall – website of Haydon Bridge High School
- Keswick School, website and conversation with Simon Jackson, Headteacher November 2014

Chapter 5 Boarding schools as charities

- Christ's Hospital history from school website and from author's diaries
- King's School, Worcester history from school website and from the author's diaries

- *The Newsom Report (1963)* '*Half Our Future'* HMSO 1963
- *The Newsom Report* (1968) '*The Public Schools Commission: First Report'* HMSO *1968*
- Graeme Paton '*Private schools claim victory in Charity Commission legal battle'* The Telegraph 14th October 2011
- Old Swinford Hospital school website and the author's diaries for External Advisor visits

Chapter 6 Royal connections

- Information about Gordon's School and the Royal Alexandra and Albert School from their school web-sites
- Colin Morrison '*Nowhere Else – the story of the Royal Wanstead School'* 1993
- '*Breaking Through – how boarding schools can transform the lives of vulnerable children'* Royal Wanstead Children's Foundation 2007

Chapter 7 The Founding of BSA and SBSA

- Tony Little's comment, from his speech to the SBSA Dinner Eton College November 2014
- 'Boarding Today' 23 Spring 2006 carried an article setting out BSA's history '*40 Years of the BSA'*
- Account of the origins of SBSA from the author's diaries

Chapter 8 Going Comprehensive

- John Haden and John Ondoma '*Oh Uganda may God uphold thee'* Barny Books 2012 provides a full account of the author's experience of teaching in Uganda set within the history of the Ugandan Church, and is available through Amazon UK as a paperback and ebook.

- Weekly boarding for 13-18 students at King Edward VI School in Morpeth was arranged by the Northumberland Local Authority on the site of the Dr Thomlinson Middle School in Rothbury although this provision no longer exists
- The Louth Plan did have similarities with the scheme for 14-18 High Schools in Leicestershire but they educated all post 14 pupils, not just the more able 25%. In Jersey, a scheme similar to the Louth Plan still exists by which more able pupils still transfer at 14+ to Hautlieu School for their 14-18 courses
- Roger Garrard and Michael Brown '*Wymondham College – the first fifty years*' WCA 2001

Chapter 9 Survival
- From diaries of the years 1992-2000 and College magazines

Chapter 10 Fit for learning and living?
- The College Chapel is still in daily use and the Memorial Garden still exists
- Group Lotus was owned until 1993 by General Motors and then by Romano Artioli who sold a majority share to Proton, a Malaysian car company; the Group Lotus business is now divided into Lotus Cars and Lotus Engineering, an engineering consultancy to the automotive industry world-wide; to have an international engineering company supporting the College's Technology and Physics departments was wonderful

Chapter 11 Academies

- Andrew Adonis *'Education, Education, Education: Reforming England's Schools'* Backbite 2012; he has been the principal advocate of State Boarding within the Academies programme

- Julian Astle and Conor Ryan (Eds) *'Academies and the Future of State Education'* Centreforum 2008 includes a foreword by Andrew Adonis, and an article on *'Boarding'* by Anthony Seldon

- Lord Nash addressed the 2013 and 2014 conferences of SBSA and has been the strongest supporter of State Boarding over the years of the Coalition Government

- Durand Academy's defence of its revenue model is set out   at https://www.gov.uk/government/uploads/system/uploads/attachment_data/file/278608/durand_-_revenue_model.pdf

Chapter 12 Specialist Schools

- The information about the Specialist schools in this chapter is mainly collected from their own web-sites, including extracts from Ofsted reports and references to the Good Schools Guide

- Ashby School boarding information from conversation with John Williams and Xenia Elias, former and current Directors of Boarding in April 2015

- Hockerill Anglo-European College information from the College web-site and from conversation with Rob Guthrie, former Principal, in March 2015

Chapter 13 6th Form boarding

- Information about Colchester RGS, Welbeck College, Peter Symonds College, and Beechen Cliff School from their respective school web-sites

- King Edward VI Grammar School boarding development from conversation with James Lascelles, Headmaster, in May 2015

Chapter 14 Overseas boarders

- Data on UK Independent boarding from the ISC Annual Census over the last five years

- Academic Asia still operates a very efficient consultancy service for Hong Kong parents and continues to help parents with British or EU to passports to access SBSA schools

Chapter 15 Teachers, Tutors and Inspectors

- Ofsted inspection of State Boarding schools remains a concern to many Heads but there is now a better understanding of such schools; where the inspection of the school's education provision and the residential inspection are both due at the same time, they are usually combined into an integrated inspection of the whole school; inspectors make judgements about the quality and effectiveness of the main areas of the school's work and how they impact the experience and outcomes of boarders or residential pupils; they check the extent to which the school has met the national minimum standards for boarding

- At that time, College Heads of House were paid on the Senior Teacher/Assistant Heads scale plus an allowance for boarding duties

- Teaching staff undertaking boarding duties were paid the relevant national teaching salary plus an allowance for boarding duties and also received free board and lodging in term-time
- 100% course-work assessment has now been stopped and replaced with controlled assessment; from 2014, all GCSE courses have been subject to 100% terminal assessment i.e. candidates are assessed at the end of their Y11 course

Chapter 16 Boarding Parents
- Garry Hinsliff *The Guardian* 20th May 2005 'Ball-bearing gun ban a step closer'

Chapter 17 Sex and Health Education
- for an amusing take on this story, see Cathy Newman *The Telegraph* 30th June 2014
- For a study of the work of those with a better Health Education budget, see Nicole Chavaudra '*The impact of virtual infant simulators in tackling under-18 conception rates in Rotherham, UK*' J Fam Plann Reprod Health Care 2007; 33(1): 35 !
- Self-examination, for both men and women. is now commonplace – in Louth in the 1980s as part of a school course, it was radical

Chapter 18 Alcohol and Drugs
- Accounts of incidents of 6th formers dying from acute alcohol poisoning continue to appear in the UK press every year, with a concentration of such cases in December and June

- A typical independent sector current school policy on 6th Form bars is *'The Sixth Form Common Room becomes a social club in the evenings after prep, with alcohol being provided on a controlled basis on Friday and Saturday evenings. The bar is managed by adults, and drinks are bought on a tab controlled by the bar manager and paid for by parents at the start of term.'*

- Cannabis remains the most popular illegal substance used by secondary school students; reports on recent studies provide many warnings but less clarity on appropriate school action; they include: Melissa Davey *The Guardian* 10th September 2014 *'Teenagers who use cannabis every day are 60% less likely to finish school'* and *'daily users under 17 are seven times more likely to commit suicide than non-users'*; Jamie Campbell *'The Independent'* 21st March 2015 *'Suspending children from school for cannabis use 'makes them more likely to reuse marijuana'*

- Having designated their schools as 'Smoking Free', Heads and Governors are now having to decide on their policy on the use of e-cigarettes, or 'vaping'; some have already followed the Welsh Assembly decision to ban all 'vaping' in a public place i.e. a school

Chapter 19 In Sickness and in Health

- The BSA has worked hard to improve the status and training of school matrons and nurses, running conferences for them, publishing briefing papers, and offering in-service training opportunities leading to professional qualifications under the leadership of Alex Thomson OBE, BSA Deputy National Director and Director of Training

- Boarding schools, having students arriving from all over the world, have to be alert to the possibility of infections from pathogens not normally found in the UK, such as bird flu, West Nile virus, ebola etc

- The training topics for this year's conference for matrons and sisters give some idea of the current concerns: Managing Difficult/Disruptive students; Sexting & Cyberbullying; Supporting the Vulnerable Student; Asthma and Schools – An Update; Self-Harming students – The Matron's role; Gender Issues in Schools; Managing students with allergies; Sex & Relationships – what difference can you make?

Chapter 20 A Vision for State Boarding?

- Two articles on the way in which boarding schools can help vulnerable children are: Melvyn Roffe, as Principal Wymondham College *'Why Assisted Boarding Works'* address to the Assisted Boarding Network Conference set up by the Buttle Trust and RHCF 20th June 2012 and DFER *'Boarding schools - An opportunity to improve outcomes for vulnerable children'* November 2014

- On 'coming out a lot': Dame Sally Coates would approve of this observation as it is one of the behaviours she advocates for Heads in *'Head Strong, 11 lessons of school leadership'* John Catt Educational 2015

- On 'you're always there': house staff including matrons are the ones to whom boarders turn when they need a listening ear and this makes the training outlined in the list of 'current concerns' above all the more important

- 'good at something': however hard it may be to find some redeeming feature in our most challenging boarders!

- The views expressed are those of the author and not necessarily endorsed by either the SBSA or the BSA

Thanks and Acknowledgements

I am very grateful to many former colleagues, current school leaders and friends for their advice, information, comments, constructive criticism and hospitality, all of which have helped with or improved this book; and especially

Rhona Adams, Stephen Bunney, Richard Davison, Xenia Elias, Muriel Grimes, Robert Guthrie, Stephen Hazlehurst, Simon Jackson, Heather Jeffrey, Peter Jones, Sam Jordison, Malcolm Kerridge, James Lascelles, Catriona Mitchell, Robert Moorhouse, John and Helen Nuttall, Martin Pearman, Clive Richardson, Melvyn Roffe, Chris Sayer, Alison Scott, Lee Smith, Paul Spencer Ellis, Simon Sprague, Jonathan Taylor, Dale Wilkins, John Williams and Peter Woodrow.

Keith Wragg's line drawings have been generously given to this project. B/W photographs are from the author's collection.

I am also grateful to innumerable boarders for providing endless examples of just how worthwhile working in boarding schools can be.

To Jenny, my wife, thank you for patience, love and timely reminders when I am tempted to take life too seriously.